The Outdoorsman
A Spiritual Survival Guide

Douglas J. Pyszka and Nelson Rhoads

Published, October 2017
Fiona Inc.
www.fionainc.com
717-917-8101

Unless otherwise identified, Bible quotations in this book are from the New King James versions of the Bible.

Copyright © 2017 Fiona Inc.
All rights reserved.
ISBN: 0-9993844-0-6
ISBN-13: 978-0-9993844-0-4

SPECIAL THANKS

Special thanks to my Lord and Savior, Jesus, Whom I love with all my heart, my Father God, who is so good to me and The Holy Spirit who has empowered me to complete this task.
A special task to my wonderful loving wife, Fiona. Her support towards me and her cooperation with me emboldens me to step out and do great and mighty things. I'm grateful to be married to such a mighty woman of God. I also want to thank my two sons, Gabriel and Josiah who have allowed me to dedicate extra time to finish this project.
A special thanks to my dad, Art, who showed me how to be an outdoorsman.
A special thanks to Nelson, an avid outdoorsman, who was my partner on this project.
Special thanks to those who helped me edit and finetuned this book. – **Douglas Pyszka**

******

I would like to thank my Lord Jesus Christ for being in my life and my dad for taking me out and enjoying the outdoors. – **Nelson Rhoads**

Contents

Introduction 1

Chapter 1 The Game Trail – the Right Path to Heaven 5

Chapter 2 The Right Spot – Finding God's Will and a Good Church 9

Chapter 3 Tracking the Right Clues – Finding Your Purpose 15

Chapter 4 Catch and Release - 19

Chapter 5 Stillness – Waiting on God 23

Chapter 6 Wear the Right Clothes – Put on Holy Garments 29

Chapter 7 Camouflage – Your Life is Hidden in Christ 35

Chapter 8 Take Good Aim – Be Like Jesus 39

Chapter 9 The Wall Hanger – Going after the Prize 45

Chapter 10 Be Aware of Your Surroundings – Know that God Loves You 51

Chapter 11 Be Prepared – Take the Right Steps of Obedience ... 57

Chapter 12 Walking Through the Darkness – Allow the Light to Lead You 61

Chapter 13 The Bait – Resist Temptation and Avoid Being Hooked 67

Chapter 14 From The Strike Zone – To the Faith Zone 73

Chapter 15 The Right Weapon and the Right Ammo – Speaking God's Word 81

Chapter 16 Keep Your Weapon Clean – Renew Your Mind 87

Chapter 17 Clean the Game – Holiness & Righteousness 93

Chapter 18 Getting the Right License – Authority of the Believer 97

Chapter 19 Calling the Game In – Assembling a Team 101

Bibliography 105

ABOUT THE AUTHORS 107

INTRODUCTION

Is there a way to discover life-changing truths about God while in the outdoors? Absolutely!

Nelson Rhoads and Douglas Pyszka are so excited to share this book with you. We are born-again, spirit-filled believers and ministers of the gospel, who love the Lord and enjoy being in the outdoors. It is our desire to communicate spiritual truths that are related to outdoor phrases. Nelson and I grew up in different places, Nelson from Pennsylvania and I from Illinois. We developed a passion for the outdoors as we both learned to hunt and fish from our fathers. We are not outdoor experts but we love and enjoy outdoor activities. It is our desire to help you to connect with God through the outdoors and so that you may know Him better.

If you are a sportsman who likes hunting and fishing or simply an outdoor enthusiast, you will appreciate the information that is revealed in this book. This is not a guide designed to teach you how to survive in the wilderness, but it is a guide that will help you survive your spiritual journey, guiding you through the wilderness of the world, and help you know the God who created the universe. This spiritual survival guide will show you godly principles that are related to outdoor terms highlighting truths that outdoorsmen are familiar with. This book will be helpful both to new believers just beginning their journey with God and to those who are well-advanced in their relationship with God.

Who is an outdoorsman? An outdoorsman is a man or woman who spends time outside enjoying activities such as camping, trapping, hunting, and fishing, and many more. Behind the outdoor terms used in this book are truths that point to the Lord Jesus Christ. Jesus Himself used parables to teach people the truths about His kingdom. A parable is a lesson about natural things like farming, herding, or grazing, that explain spiritual truths. This book is full of outdoor parables that explain truths about God's kingdom.

God is an awesome Creator who created this world that we live in by speaking what He wanted into existence. Creation points to a Creator. God, who made the natural world, can also teach you things about Himself through the world He made. It takes faith to understand all that God made and how He made it (Hebrews 11:3). The Bible says that the heavens and the earth declare the glory of God (Psalms 19:1). Outdoorsmen love doing their favorite activities outside because the earth was made for man to enjoy.

Many people can connect with God by being outdoors because creation declares God's glory and shows His handiwork (Psalm 19:1). The earth is full of the glory of God. The outdoors contains evidence that God exists and He is working in the earth. The prophet Isaiah recorded that the whole earth is full of God's glory (Isaiah 6:3). The psalmist said that God laid the foundation of the earth, and the heavens are the work of His hands (Ps 102:25). All outdoorsmen need to open their hearts and learn some things about God through the natural world.

According to the Bible, you can even learn something from observing an ant, a very small creature in nature (Proverbs 6:1). Ants can organize, carry out instructions and accomplish great things even though they are very small in size. They have no leader yet thrive in many different environments. If you can learn lessons from an ant, you can also learn many other things about God from the outdoors.

We celebrate every outdoor enthusiast and we hope that the truths revealed in this book will enhance your life, equip you with tools to be successful, aid you on your spiritual journey and help you to know more about God, His work, and His kingdom. This is a guide to help you understand the God who created nature by using natural terms to teach spiritual truths. If you are a person who loves the outdoors and desires to learn more about Jesus from examples found in the natural world, then this will be a useful tool for you. God will enrich your knowledge of Him so you can grow in Christianity. Ask the Lord to help you understand what He is saying and glean from the truths that are unveiled in this book.

PYSZKA AND RHOADS

CHAPTER 1
THE GAME TRAIL – THE RIGHT PATH TO HEAVEN

Is there a right path that leads to heaven? Discover the game trail that leads to God.

Anyone who spends a good amount of time in the outdoors, especially wooded areas, will come across game trails. Game trails are well-traveled paths that animals use to hunt, graze, and find what they need to live on and survive. These paths lead from an animal's lair to its livelihood.

Consider how deer make trails. When a deer finds a reliable feeding ground or watering hole, it will use the same path or trail continually to get to these places that are necessary for its life. Walking on this trail becomes a main part of the deer's daily routine. The grass that once covered the ground on these trails becomes worn down, and only a dirt trail remains. Some animals use game trails to hunt other animals that travel on those paths.

While game trails are predominantly used by animals, humans have found them handy as well. Hikers that wander from a marked trail or get lost might be able to follow a well-trodden game trail to a waterway, which could then eventually lead to civilization.
These paths can be used as shortcuts, or they can be a way to pass through otherwise impassable terrain.

Game trails prove that animals are in the area or they frequently pass through the area. Clues left on the trail - fur, tracks, feces, disheveled greenery, and marks, like rubs on trees - reveal the types of animals that use that trail. If you come across a game trail, look closely at these signs. Hunters can set up a stand or a blind near a game trail in hopes of catching the animals that travel on that path. Researchers can use game trails to track species that are present in an area to monitor their health or any changes in population. A game trail is a sign that animals are present, and the clues you find along the trail reveal what type of animals you may encounter.

After you find a game trail, you should be able to track the animals that use it. Tracking animals is the art of interpreting signs like footprints, fur, and nibbled plants to discover who has recently been foraging, hunting, evading danger or resting in a certain area. A tracker sees details that others may miss. A tracker follows the clues that animals leave behind. The clues you find on the game trail are important in determining what types of animals you may face. Follow the clues and interpret the signs, and you will find what you are looking for.

One time, Nelson was hunting deer near a fox hole. He saw signs on a trail that showed deer were traveling there. After waiting a long time without seeing any deer, he gave up and decided to try another location. There were no deer at the new location, so he went back to the trail that he originally discovered. He was surprised to find fresh fur and a fresh scrape on a tree near the fox hole. The size of the marks showed that a big buck had been there while he was gone. He learned not to travel too far from a game trail because he missed out on what could have been a great reward.

You have a description of what a game trail is in the natural, but what is the game trail for a Christ follower? What can a Christian learn from game trails? **The game trail**

for a Christ follower is the path that leads to life and to heaven, and there is only one. The only way that leads to heaven is the path that leads you into a relationship with Jesus Christ. Jesus described Himself as being the way, the only way to God (John 14:6). There are not many ways or even several ways to God; there is only one way to God. This word "way" that describes Jesus means "a road, a route, or a means to something." (1) **The Bible describes the believer's game trail as a path of life (Psalms 16:11). The path of life takes you into God's presence and leads you to joy if you follow it.**

The way to heaven is heavily traveled, just like a game trail you may find in the wilderness. Many people have found this way and discovered eternal life. There are also many who have yet to discover this trail. Jesus not only paved this way for us, but He also left clues on this path to show that this is the right way. Here are some of the clues you may find on this path:

- Jesus' perfect, sinless life
- The miracles He performed
- Lessons He taught
- The lives that were changed by Him
- The cross He died on
- The empty tomb He resurrected from.

These clues point to Jesus as being the one and only Son of God and true Savior of mankind. Have you discovered the path to Jesus? Do you recognize the clues that point to Jesus? Insert chapter one text here. Insert chapter one text here. Insert chapter one text here. Insert chapter one text here.

Jesus is the only name that brings salvation (Acts 4:12). Salvation comes only through Jesus Christ. God made Jesus the Prince and Savior of everyone who accepts Him. To enjoy the benefits of everlasting life, you must believe in Jesus as your Savior and accept Him as your Lord. Jesus is the only one qualified to be your Savior. He is God's Son, born of a virgin, was tempted in all ways that humans are tempted in, but He never sinned.

Only a sinless Savior could rescue others from the dominion of sin. He gave His life as a ransom for many. God demonstrated His perfect love for you by sacrificing Jesus on the cross. That is where sin's debt was cancelled. His resurrection is proof He is who He said He was. Jesus is the only one qualified to save mankind, and the path that leads you to Jesus is the right path, the only path of life.

If you want to follow this godly game trail, decide to surrender your life to God. Believe in Jesus, accept Him, confess Him as your Lord, and continue to follow Him your whole life. Allow God's Holy Spirit to bring you into truth and teach you about the Bible. The path that leads to Jesus is the only path that leads to eternal life. **Forsaking this path and going in a direction opposite of where Jesus is will cost you greatly.** Other paths that do not lead to Jesus end up in darkness, torment, and hell forever. God gives you the ability to choose your path. Choose wisely, for only one leads to life. Get on the life-giving path today.

CHAPTER 2
THE RIGHT SPOT – FINDING GOD'S WILL AND A GOOD CHURCH

Can I find God's will and a good church, and are they the right spot for me?

There is an expression that fishermen use to describe a location where fish are easily caught in abundance called "the right spot." You could also call a place like this a hot spot for fishing. Fishermen long to find a place like this because the fishing activity is intense and fun. Here, fish are usually caught one after the other.

Several years ago, I (Doug) was fishing with my friends in a lake in Illinois. As all fishermen do, we were hoping for a good catch, but didn't imagine just how good of a catch we had stumbled upon. We discovered a spawning bed for crappie, the place where the fish came to reproduce and lay their eggs. It was a hot spot! Every time I cast my line into the water, I caught a fish. My friends and I were pulling in fish after fish. They just kept coming in. These were good-sized crappie. In the end, we had filled four collapsible baskets full of fish. We were amazed and excited. Discovering the right spot made all the difference.

The right spot is a place that provides the greatest rewards for fishermen. It is where they catch the most fish. Sometimes it takes great effort, much time and steadfast patience and persistence to find the right spot, but discovering the right spot is worth it. A fisherman may try several places before finding the right spot. A boat is a helpful tool in finding the right spot because it allows you to easily maneuver in the water. It is more difficult to find the right spot from land because a fisherman has to move by foot in search of it.

Some fishermen fish in rivers and streams. This type of fishing involves a lot of walking. In smaller bodies of water there may be only a few select places that are good for catching fish. Over a stretch of many miles, there may be only a few deep holes where fish gather. However, when the right place is found, the fisherman stays there and catches as many fish as possible, then moves on. He must strike when the fishing is hot. Finding the right spot, in whatever type of fishing you do, is a great joy.

One night, while night-fishing, Nelson discovered a hot spot as he was wading in the water. Nelson was fishing with lures. As he was reeling his line in, something hit it very hard. The fish put up a good fight. Finally, he reeled the fish in and much to his surprise, there were two bass hooked on one lure. What a great catch. The fishing was so good, he fished until midnight.

You now know what the right spot for fishing is but what is the "right spot" for a Christ follower? If you have faith in Jesus Christ as Lord, then the right spot for you is to know and do God's will and be part of a good church. God wants you to know His will for your life, and He will connect you with a good church that will help you find His will for you. You will find that doing God's will as a Christian is as rewarding as a fisherman finding the right spot. Fulfilling God's will for your life directs you to receive all that He promised you (Hebrews 10:36). **Your richest rewards and greatest joy will come from doing what God wants you to do in life. That is your right spot where you can draw**

on and receive God's best.

The other part of the right spot is finding the right church. What is the church? The church is not the building but the people who come together to praise the Lord. The church is carrying out the work that Jesus initiated. God designed His church to be the right place for believers to gather together, to gain knowledge and wisdom, to learn about Jesus, to grow, to develop in faith, and to experience God's power by His Holy Spirit. The church is the right spot where a Christ follower can catch great things from God.

The church is important to Jesus because He is the CEO of the church; He created it, bought it with His blood, and is building it up now. Jesus promised to build His church, and hell cannot stop it (Matthew 16:18). The church consists of believers in two locations: on earth and in heaven. God inspired and instructed writers like Paul, Peter, James, and John to write letters to the church to instruct and guide its members. The church is very important to the Lord, and it should be important to every believer in Christ.

Allow God to put you in a church that He desires, one that teaches and preaches the Word of God and allows His Spirit to move, manifest, and work. There you can learn about God's will, grow in your knowledge of God, and receive the benefits by applying His principles to your life. It is very important to find your hot spot in the Lord which is God's will and your place in His church. Becoming a faithful and active member of the church that God places you in is a big part of doing His will for your life. **When you find your hot spot, you can receive great rewards in life.** Find your hot spot today and God will bless you for it.

God wants you to know His will, so He mapped it out for you in His Word (Colossians 1:9). You cannot do God's will without knowing what His will is. The Bible is the right place and really the only place where God's will can be discovered. God's Holy Spirit is available to help guide you into God's perfect will. God also employs His church, made up of His people, as an institution designed to promote His will in the earth. A good church will instruct people about God.

It is God's will to bring people out of things that are bad, dangerous, destructive and oppressive and into something that is good, beneficial, wholesome, and life-giving. Sin, disobedience to God's will, is the cause of all these types of bad things. In the Bible, God brought His people, Israel, out of Egypt, a representation of sin. He took them out of Egypt and brought them into something much better, a good, rich, fertile land that would belong to them (Exodus 3:8). **The will of God always improves and increases your life.** It is always for your good and designed to be rewarding to you. When you know and do God's will you can experience growth, abundance, protection, provision, and plenty.

You may be wondering, "How do I locate and carry out God's will?" Make a wholehearted decision to accept Jesus as your Lord and continue to follow Him your whole life. Be willing to make God's agenda your highest priority. Read and study the Bible, and be part of a good church that teaches it fully.

Just as fishermen are equipped to catch different fish, God has equipped everyone who follows the Lord Jesus with everything they need to do His will (Hebrews 13:21). At times a fisherman may use specialized tools such as electronic fish finders or a GPS to locate fish. These tools can help a fisherman find the right spot. God also equips believers with specialized tools from His Holy Spirit, who is your personal GPS guide to help lead you into God's perfect will. He will show you where to go and what to do. He will guide you on your journey and help you along the way.

Another way to discover God's will is to ask Him what He wants; He will teach you (Psalm 143:10). He is eager, willing, and capable of helping you find the right spot. Jesus found His right spot, God's will for Him, when He opened the book of Isaiah 61:1-2 and declared what He came to do. God wanted Jesus to preach, to heal, to proclaim liberty, to set captives free, to promote God's kingdom, to comfort and console mourners, to bring beauty out of ashes, and to save mankind from sin. Luke 19:10 tells us that Jesus came to seek and save the lost. Jesus is our example, so if Jesus knew the Father's will, you can know it too. Ask God to reveal His plan for your life, and enjoy life in the right spot from this day on. The next chapter will give you some tools to discovering God's purpose for your life.

CHAPTER 3
TRACKING THE RIGHT CLUES – FINDING YOUR PURPOSE

Does God have a divine purpose for me, and can I discover what it is easily?

This chapter will help you further to find God's will for your just like a game trail points to the presence of animals. If an outdoorsman wants to find his game, he must be able to track his game. Tracking animals is an important skill that an outdoorsman needs to develop. An outdoorsman is excited when he discovers a footprint in the mud or snow. Every animal has a distinct print that varies in size, the number of toes and whether it has claws or hooves. If you know what to look for, you'll be able to tell what type of animal might be nearby.

There are three main methods an outdoorsman may employ in tracking animals: identification, interpretation, and following the animals themselves. First, you must identify any animal tracks you see to know if it is the right animal. You can identify an animal when you properly interpret the clues and signs the animal leaves behind. After you identify an animal using these three methods, you can follow it across the terrain. Tracking is a very good skill that an outdoorsman needs to have.

Just as an outdoorsman uses three main methods to track animals and catch them, as a Christ follower, you are identifying, interpreting and following **your divine purpose**. When God created you, He made you on purpose for a purpose. God has an assignment for every person, problems to solve, and things to do on this earth. God helps His followers to find their purpose by the instructions He gives them. There are clues and signs you will find as you communicate with God that point out your purpose. When you find what God has created you for, you will have true joy that overflows.

How to Find Your Purpose – Identify, Interpret and Follow

God helps you find your purpose through His Word, His Spirit, and His angels. Believers in Christ can also use the same methods that outdoorsmen use: identification, interpretation, and following. If you want to find your purpose, first identify how God speaks to you. You will learn how He speaks to you as you spend time with Him. If Jesus is your Lord, you are one of His sheep, and you can become familiar with hearing His voice (John 10:4).

Once you know His voice, you can then interpret what He is saying through the Bible. When you know the author of a book you can truly understand what he is saying in his book. God's Word is forever settled in heaven and it does not need to be changed or added to. The more familiar you become with the book God wrote, the easier it is to understand what He is saying to you. His Word is alive. As you identify God's voice and interpret what He said, you can follow Him wherever He directs. Following comes after identifying and interpreting.

If Jesus is your Lord, then He gets to direct your life. You can only find your purpose by being connected to Jesus. Only God knows why you were created. You can only discover your destiny as you track the clues and signs that

God leaves you every day.

Here are three very important clues that God has left for you.
- God speaks to you with His voice. His sheep know and follow His voice (John 10:3-4).
- God leads you by His Spirit (Romans 8:14).
- God has given you His Word as a lamp to guide your way (Psalms 119:105).

God will even help direct you to hunt. The Lord helped Nelson improve his hunting skills by showing him, through a vision, where deer would enter an area and how they would travel to different places. As the Lord showed him these things, Nelson would set up in the spot the Lord showed him. He was ready to get a deer because he allowed God to lead, guide and direct him. He got his deer because he followed God.

Colossians 1:9-12 contains some very important clues to finding your divine purpose.

> *"9 For this reason also, since the day we heard of it, we have not ceased to pray for you and to ask **that you may be filled with the knowledge of His will** in all spiritual wisdom and understanding, 10 so that you will walk in a manner worthy of the Lord, to please Him in all respects, bearing fruit in every good work and increasing in the knowledge of God; 11 strengthened with all power, according to His glorious might, for the attaining of all steadfastness and patience; joyously 12 giving thanks to the Father, who has qualified us to share in the inheritance of the saints in Light."*

What clues do we find here that will lead us to discovering our destiny?

- Clue 1- Pray and ask God to show you what His will is for you (V. 9).
- Clue 2 - God will give you wisdom and understanding that will help you know His plan for you (V.9).
- Clue 3- God created you, called you, and equipped you, so make it your goal to please Him and carry out His plan (V.10).
- Clue 4 - Your purpose progresses and expands as you walk with God (V. 10).
- Clue 5 – God gives you strength, might and power to carry out His will (V. 11).
- Clue 6 – You will find that God's purpose is satisfying you and you will be thankful that God qualified you for an inheritance.

Knowing these clues, you can successfully track your purpose, just like the hunter who tracks the big game. **Use God's strength, skill, and steadfast patience to find your purpose and fulfill it.**

CHAPTER 4
CATCH AND RELEASE -
THINGS YOU THOUGHT YOU WANTED BUT COULD DO WITHOUT

When I become a Christian is there anything that I should dispose of?

Catch-and-release is a method of fishing in which the fish that are caught are released after capture as a conservation measure. This approach allows an outdoorsman to see what he caught. If, after close inspection, he realizes that what he caught was not what he wanted to keep, he releases it back in the water. There are also some fishermen who like the sport of fishing, but they may not eat fish or like to clean them, so they practice this method called catch-and-release.

The catch-and-release principle also applies to hunting but it is carried out in a different way. A hunter may have game he is ready to catch, because it is in his sights, and he is ready to shoot. He releases the animal by not shooting it if he sees that it is too small or not the right gender. Some hunting licenses are gender specific, and the hunter can only shoot the gender that his license permits. Releasing an animal back into the wild when hunting is a choice between shooting it or not shooting it. Releasing a fish after it has been caught is easier than releasing an animal after it has been shot because fish are not seriously injured when caught. On the other hand, when an animal is shot in hunting is probably injured severely or already dead.

You have seen how the catch-and-release method works in the outdoors, but how can a Christ follower implement the catch-and-release principle in his or her life?

If you "catch" Christ, receiving Him into your heart, the way you think and act changes. When you look at your old attitudes, mindsets, and beliefs, you will realize that you do not need them anymore. They are no longer adequate, necessary, or fit for Christ followers. Now is the time to release them back into the world. If you are a Christian you must throw back your old attitudes, mindsets, and beliefs because they are unnecessary to you. The Lord changes your attitudes, mindsets and beliefs into better things. You keep the better things and release the old things.

When you become a Christian, you will have many catch-and-release moments. In those moments, you get to choose what to keep and what you should let go. Here are some things to catch and release when you become a Christian:

- Catch eternal life and release death. Eternal life is worth holding on to.
- Embrace victory and throw back defeat. Have faith in Jesus for He gives you the victory.
- Catch a willing and obedient heart for Jesus, and throw back disobedience to God.
- Catch praising the Lord, and release exalting yourself. Honor God with praise, and stop magnifying yourself.
- Catch the light of God, and throw back the darkness. Walk in the light; it helps you find your way easier.
- Catch a holy, pure, and clean life for God, and give up immorality, uncleanness, and greed. Living for God is living according to a higher standard.

- Catch truthfulness, and release all lying. Be truthful in all things, and do not lie.
- Catch self-control and release anger from consuming you. Don't let anger stifle your self-control; follow God not the devil. You can be angry at evil and yet keep your dignity.
- Catch kindness, tenderness, and forgiveness, and release all bitterness, wrath, anger, clamor, and evil (Ephesians 2:1-3; 4:17-32).

When Jesus is Lord, He leads, guides and directs you by His Word and Spirit. Your new life in Christ requires you to catch a higher life and release your lower life (Colossians 3).

Implementing the catch-and-release principle in your life is about making right choices. If you caught something that you do not like or do not want, or something the Lord leads you to give up, then you choose to give it up and release your hold on it. Catch the things that God gives you and hold onto them. Release the things that God leads you to release. God will help you exchange all the bad things in your life, for all the good things that He gives you.

The new things that God gives you are best for you, and you can cherish His gifts forever. Catch the Lord's abundant life, made up of love, joy, compassion, kindness, humility, gentleness, forgiveness and patience. Release your sinful life, the nature of the enemy, made up of sexual immorality, impurity, evil desires and idolatry, rage, malice, slander and filthy language (Galatians 5). For a Christ follower, Jesus is Lord and Master so you must catch His nature and a way of doing things. **Your former master was Satan, and you want to get rid of anything resembling him.** God by His Spirit and Word will help you catch what is good and release what was bad.

The degree to which you accept God's Word in your heart and follow His Spirit is the degree to which you will implement it in your life (James 1:19-25). As a Christian, your desires and appetites change from sinfulness and selfishness to putting Christ first. You desire better things that enhance your walk with the Lord such as the pure spiritual milk, God's Word, that helps you grow in your salvation (1 Peter 2:1-3). Christianity produces different fruit because it has its roots in the right soil (Galatians 5:16-26).

The closer you are to Jesus Christ, the more you realize that the things of the world are less important to you. Hold onto Jesus and never let Him go. The Bible tells you in James 1:21 to humbly receive or **catch** God's Word, and to lay aside, or **release** wickedness. God gives you the ability and the freedom to choose which life you want to embrace. You can embrace a good life in God that will last forever, or you can choose to embrace a bad life, without God, and be tormented in darkness forever. You are intelligent, so take hold of God and **let things that are unnecessary go.**

CHAPTER 5
STILLNESS – WAITING ON GOD

How long do I have to wait on God? What do I get for waiting on God?

The outdoors can be a peaceful and tranquil place. Many outdoorsmen enjoy the sights and sounds they encounter in the wilderness because it helps them clear their minds and calm their souls. The best way to enjoy this atmosphere is to be still, quiet, and motionless. When you are still, you are more in tune with the sights and sounds you may experience in an outdoor setting.

Develop the art of being still to enhance your outdoor experience. Often hunters must be still and wait for game to come in range so they can get the best shot. Fishing also can be a waiting game as a fisherman waits for fish to seize the bait. Once a trapper sets a trap, the only thing he can do is wait till the trap is sprung. Waiting patiently for something you cannot control, like the behavior of animals, takes discipline, practice and self-control.

The senses of animals are far superior to human senses. They can hear better, see movement better and have a better sense of smell to detect different scents. Because animals are so keen in their senses, outdoorsmen must be skilled at being still. Some movements and sounds can scare prey away. Remaining still is even more difficult in extreme temperatures, especially when it is cold.

Even the animal kingdom knows the value of waiting. Many predators in the animal kingdom wait, silent and still, until they can capture prey. Spiders are trappers that wait for prey to get stuck in their web. Alligators remain hidden and wait to strike at the right moment. Lions stalk their prey by crouching, moving slow and waiting until they can pounce on their prey to devour them. Many animals are highly skilled in being still and waiting.

One time, Nelson was using a blind to hunt deer that his friend normally used. The wind was blowing heavily which made it difficult to pinpoint exactly where other sounds were coming from. Also, acorns were falling and Nelson could hear them hit the ground. Nelson was alerted to a different and distinct sound, the sound of a branch cracking as something had stepped on it, and it made his chest burn with excitement. He was not sure where it came from. He then turned quickly, with his bow ready, and a doe was coming from the thicket behind him. He learned to wait and listen for a clear sound.

As you wait and are still, you become more in tune with your surroundings and are more likely to snag your reward. On the other hand, failing to wait properly can cause you to miss out on a great prize.

One time, when I (Doug) was much younger, I was deer hunting with a bow from an open tree stand. Many hours had passed and I had not seen any deer where I was, even though there were visible signs that they often passed through there. Needless to say, I fell asleep. It was not for long, but when I awoke, there were three deer within twenty yards and I had a clear shot. However, because I fell asleep, I was not ready to shoot. I fumbled with my arrow to place it on the string, and when I pulled the bow back it made a noise and the deer took off in a hurry. I did not get a shot off and was disappointed because I had missed a great opportunity.

An outdoorsman should be patient, still, alert, and ready because the right opportunity can come unexpectedly. He should wait for prey as if he is guarding something valuable. Just as a guard would be in trouble for sleeping on duty, a hunter can miss his target if he falls asleep.

You have seen the importance of being still and waiting in the outdoors but what does it mean to be still and wait for a Christ follower? To be still for a Christian means to quiet the mind and senses and tune into to God's voice because He speaks within a person, in the heart of a believer. It also means to be free from distractions and focused on God. What does a Christian wait for? Waiting for a Christian means listening for God to speak, instruct, lead, and guide. As a Christian, it is important to know how to be still and wait.

Waiting on God renews your strength and helps you overcome challenges (Isaiah 40:31). Christians should wait on the Lord with patience and expectation, and they should focus their attention on what God is saying in the moment. Failing to wait on the Lord causes you to act presumptuously and miss God's best. If a Christian cannot be still and wait on God, he or she will fail to attain the prize.

The Bible says in Psalms 46:10, "Be still and know that God is God." Stillness increases knowledge and awareness. Distractions disappear when you are still, and you can hear God's voice more clearly and understand what He is saying better. Stillness creates a peaceful and pleasant atmosphere so you can focus on the task at hand, achieving your goal, or receiving something from God.

Waiting on God means being ready to act and serve Him when He speaks. Waiting requires a willing and obedient participant. When God shows you something, He only shows you a part of His plan. You must act in faith and do what He shows you if you want to know the next part. Once you do your part you must wait on Him to reveal the next step. **Waiting on God and not getting ahead of Him could be the difference between crossing the finish line victoriously or not crossing it at all.** Waiting on God takes a good heart and a strong determination (Psalm 27:14).

It takes discipline, self-denial and self-control to be still and patiently wait successfully.

There are many things that are out of your control in the wilderness. You will have to deal with some things like boredom, extreme weather and being uncomfortable to be still and wait for the prize. Your body will want to move away from these things but you can train your body to endure all circumstances until you achieve the goal. Patience is worthy to be pursued (1 Timothy 6:11). Patience and faith work together to help you receive what God promised. Be still and wait with readiness for the right opportunity.

Every Christ follower must also resist things that come against them when they are in waiting mode, for example, the flesh, negative circumstances, and the enemy and his evil spirits. The way you resist these things is to speak God's Word with your mouth and believe it in your heart. Because the essence of faith is to wait patiently on God, it is the goal of your enemy to stop you from waiting, and so get you out of faith.

You must trust in God to wait on God (Isaiah 8:17). God is a person who cannot lie, does not change, and does not need to do things over because He made a mistake. God never has nor ever will make a mistake. You can trust in His nature and character because He will not fail you. Wait on Him and wait for Him to move on your behalf with words to encourage you and His strength to turn your circumstances around.

God Himself is patient. The Bible in Romans 15:5 describes God as the God of patience and comfort. Also, James said that God has great patience for the precious fruit of the earth (James 5:7). What that means is God waits for people to hear His message and come to the knowledge of the truth that Jesus is Lord of all.

Waiting is an important trait in Christianity. God Himself waits patiently for people to accept His gift of salvation (James 5:7). His followers are waiting patiently for the Lord to return. The ability to be still and patiently wait is a biblical principle for every believer in Christ Jesus and it is also a principle for every outdoorsman who enjoys the outdoors. As an outdoorsman hangs in there and waits for the right opportunity so must the Christian hang in there and be patient to endure challenges. Patience turns challenges into opportunities and good testimonies. If you can develop this skill you will be rewarded greatly. Do not be in a hurry but wait, watch and listen to the Lord. God will do great things for you.

CHAPTER 6
WEAR THE RIGHT CLOTHES – PUT ON HOLY GARMENTS

Do I have the right clothing and the right equipment to be a Christian?

It is important for every outdoorsman to wear the right clothes and possess the right equipment to be able to get the game they are after. Clothing and equipment is a big cost to the outdoorsman. There are different things to consider that will determine what you wear and what gear you may need.

- Every outdoor activity you choose to participate in - whether you hunt, fish or rock climb, just to name a few - will determine what you wear and what equipment you need.
- Another factor to consider is the climate. Different places have different climates. Climates can be hot, cold, dry, damp, and snow-covered. What you wear in these places makes a big difference.
- A third factor to consider in choosing the right attire is the setting your activity takes place in. If your interest puts you in the desert, the mountains, thick woods, or a swamp, you will need to adjust what you wear for each place.
- A fourth factor to think about is the type of terrain that you will be walking on. You will need different

shoes to handle different types of terrain.

• Lastly, consider the proper equipment you will need to support the outdoor activity you are involved in. Hunters, fisherman, and climbers will use different gear to go along with their different clothing.

• Hunters need things like weapons, ammo, and licenses to hunt; fishermen need poles, nets, tackle, a knife, and a license to fish; and climbers need harnesses, ropes, carabiners, spikes and other accessories to climb.

It is necessary for outdoorsmen to have the right clothing and equipment to get the most out of their endeavors in the outdoors.

Just as an outdoorsman should have the right clothing and equipment, a Christ follower should also have the right clothing and equipment to follow Jesus Christ. You may be wondering, what exactly does a Christian wear? Christians wear clothing that cannot necessarily be seen with the natural eye, but it is very real. The clothes worn by Christians are spiritual attributes that can be put on like a garment.

The spiritual garments worn by Christians are not purchased in a store. God is the one who provides His followers with the right clothing and equipment to wear. When God created man, Adam, He placed him and his wife, Eve, in a garden. God had a good relationship with them. Everything was great until man disobeyed God's command and sinned. Sin caused the relationship between God and man to be broken. Adam and Eve were full of guilt and shame, and they tried to cover themselves with leaves (Genesis 3:7). The clothes that were made from leaves were not sufficient to cover their sin. God Himself clothed Adam and Eve with animal skins (Genesis 3:21). God made a sacrifice to cover man's sin. This foreshadowed the sacrifice that Jesus would make to cover our sin.

The Bible says **God clothes His priests** with salvation (Psalm 132:16). Salvation is described as clothing that can be put on. God calls His children kings and priests (Revelation 1:6). Being clothed with salvation causes you to rejoice and be glad, and it is literally, putting on Christ. That means you take on His nature and you live life differently. Being clothed with salvation is necessary to function in God's kingdom.

Another piece of clothing that God gives to His followers to wear is the robe of righteousness (Isaiah 61:10). Having faith in Jesus as Lord immediately gives you access to this tailor-made robe. Wearing this robe, you will be stunning as a bridegroom who is dressed in a sharp suit on his wedding day. The robe of righteousness is necessary to go into God's presence. It makes you clean, holy, and pure. God, your Creator, designed it for you after the pattern of His Son Jesus. It is designed to be worn daily and will last forever.

Two books in the Bible, Ephesians 2 and Colossians 3, both tell us to "put on the new man," which is a phrase that describes what you do with clothing. The new man is the nature of Christ, created in righteousness and true holiness. It is a spiritual attribute a Christ follower can wear. You could say that righteousness and holiness are the threads that make the new man garment. Just like an outdoorsman puts on his boots, pants, and shirt to go outdoors, a Christian can put on the new man and to live a righteous and holy life.

God has a uniform, called the armor of God (Ephesians 6:10-18). God gives this armor to identify, equip, and protect His saints must like every branch of the military has a uniform to identify, equip, and protect their soldiers. This armor is made up of a helmet of salvation, a breastplate of righteousness, a belt of truth, shoes of readiness, a sword of the spirit, and a shield of faith. These items of clothing are designed to identify, equip and protect every saint to accomplish his divine mission and gain the victory. As a Christ follower, you can wear this armor like you would any other clothing.

God has even provided you with a special garment, called the garment of praise, to wear when you are feeling down or you have a heavy heart (Isaiah 61:3). This garment inspires you to praise the Lord and it causes sorrow and depression to leave you. Put on your tailor-made garment of praise that will help you to be joyful.

You must be prepared for the different environments you may find yourself in. The world we live in today is a harsh environment full of sin, suffering, pain, destruction, and death. Heaven is a much different environment than this world. A person who has not accepted Jesus as Lord is a sinner, wearing a filthy garment that stinks, is stained, and looks bad. God wants to replace the filthy garment with one that He made that is clean and holy (Zechariah 3:3-5). Just as a filthy sin garment denies you access into heaven, God's garment gives you access. You must change garments so that you are prepared to overcome the harsh environment of sin and live a new life in Christ.

The Bible tells a story of a son who demanded to receive his inheritance early, before his father died. After getting his inheritance, he left his family and went out on his own to experience the world and what it offered (Luke 15). The son spent his money on worldly pleasures and soon it was gone. He was broke, and the only job he could get was feeding pigs. He was so hungry that he desired to eat what the pigs ate. If a person thinks what a pig eats is good, that person has hit rock bottom.

The man decided to return home to simply serve his wealthy father. The father saw his son a great distance away, and ran to him, embraced him, and forgave him. He ordered his servants to **put a new robe on his son**. They removed his filthy smelly garments and replaced them with a new, clean and fresh-smelling robe.

This is a picture of how God wants to clothe you. If you do not know Jesus Christ as Lord you are wearing the wrong clothing, and you need to change. God has tailor-made holy garments for you that are necessary to enter heaven's atmosphere. If you accept Jesus as your Lord and invite Him into your heart then you can put on the clothes that God has provided for you.

CHAPTER 7
CAMOUFLAGE – YOUR LIFE IS HIDDEN IN CHRIST

How can I be camouflaged from the world and how can I hide in Christ?

There is something that is excellently designed to conceal things in the outdoors. This tool is utilized by both humans and animals, and is called camouflage. The skin and coats of animals naturally help them blend in with their environments. Being able to be concealed helps animals in two ways: it helps predators to sneak up on prey without being seen, and it also helps prey to hide from predators. Humans also have developed camouflage clothing that helps them blend in so animals do not notice them. Hunters who can conceal themselves have a greater chance of getting game to come within range. Camouflage helps you to conceal your location, disguise your appearance, and hide your presence.

You can see how important camouflage is in the outdoors, but how can camouflage benefit a Christ follower? The camouflage for the Christian is Christ Jesus Himself. Christians **blend in** to a righteous environment by confessing Jesus as Lord and taking on His nature, characteristics, and mannerisms.

Before a man comes to Christ, he is bound by sin, a slave to sin, and has a sin nature. Sin exposes him to the devil giving him an opportunity to steal, kill, and destroy as he pleases. On the other hand, a believer who is in Christ is cleansed and freed from sin by the blood of Jesus, and he or she is **camouflaged**. A Christ follower has the old sin nature removed and is given a new nature which makes him look like Jesus (2 Corinthians 5:17). With his life hidden in Christ, he can now avoid being devoured God's enemy.

Putting on Christ makes you like a hunter who puts on camouflage to be concealed in the wilderness: you can be so well hidden that you are unrecognizable. The Bible reveals how the apostle Paul was converted. His name was Saul until Jesus changed his name to Paul. Saul persecuted Christ followers, threatened them, arrested them, imprisoned them, and consented to their death. Then one day, Paul met Jesus on his way to Damascus (Acts 9:4-6). He became a Christian and His life was changed forever.

Paul illustrates in (Galatians 2:20) how his life was camouflaged in Christ and how that impacted him. Paul testified that he was crucified with Christ and he no longer lived. He was so disguised in Christ that people could not see the terrorist that he once was. Paul determined that the life he lived after meeting Christ, would be carried out by faith in God. If you lived in Paul's day and knew him before and after Christ, you would think that Paul looked more like Jesus than he looked like Saul. Saul was his old nature while Paul was his new nature. When you are hidden in Christ your mistakes, faults, and sins are no longer recognizable. They no longer define you; instead, Christ defines you. Put on your Christian camouflage today.

According to Colossians 3:3, being hidden in God is the result of dying to self. You no longer run your life as you see fit; instead, you surrender to the lordship of Jesus and allow Him to direct your life. Pleasing Christ becomes the most important priority in your life. When your life is hidden in

Christ, your physical senses cease to control your thoughts and actions, and you live by faith in God. When you do what Christ commands, you take on his nature. His life becomes your life, and you are camouflaged in Him. Get hidden in Christ today.

CHAPTER 8
TAKE GOOD AIM – BE LIKE JESUS

Can I really live a life like Jesus lived?

When an outdoorsman has his target in range and in his sight, he must take **good aim** by raising his weapon, pointing it at the target, staying focused, and taking the shot. The ability to aim at and hit a target is a good skill for a hunter to possess.

Here are a few simple tips to help you fire a weapon effectively and accurately.

- First, get a good grip on the weapon, whether it is a rifle, pistol, or a bow.
- Secondly, raise it up and point it at the target.
- Thirdly, release the safety, pull back the hammer, or pull the bow string back.
- Finally, look at your target, placing the bead at the end of the barrel or the arrowhead on the target. Then take a deep breath and exhale slowly as you squeeze the trigger or release the bow string.

It is necessary for you to practice these steps to develop and improve your shooting skill.

If you use different weapons, whether guns or bows, keep your shooting skills sharp by taking target practice often.

Law enforcement agents, all branches of the military and outdoorsmen, have regular target practice at gun ranges to maintain their aiming skill. People in these groups practice drawing their weapons from their holsters and shooting from different distances and positions to be able hit a target when it is in sight. A good shooter who often hits a bullseye is called a marksman. If you want to increase your accuracy, practice your aiming skills.

When I was in high school, I worked for a gun club and saw firsthand how shooters practiced taking good aim. The club met monthly on a Saturday and Sunday to shoot pistols at black metal targets, in the shape of different animals. Each animal was set at a different distance - chickens were at twenty-five yards; turkeys were at fifty yards, pigs were at seventy-five yards, and rams were at a hundred yards. All the target-setters sat in a bunker with a radio. The shooters would shoot for two minutes, then unload their guns and call us on the radio to say, "All clear." We then ran out on the field, set the targets up that were knocked down, painted them, and ran back to the bunker. We radioed base to notify them that we were clear. Working at that gun club showed me the importance of taking aim in hitting the target.

Just as an outdoorsman should take good aim to be able to shoot animals accurately and effectively, a Christ follower should take good aim at seeking the Lord, a higher life in Christ Jesus and those things that are above - righteousness, godliness and holiness.
(1 Chronicles 22:19; Colossians 3:1-5). Your target practice, is being like Jesus in your thoughts, words, attitudes, and actions. Set up God's Word before your eyes like an outdoorsman sets up practice targets and develop your skill by being Christlike.

Every Christian should have Jesus in their sights by getting a good hold on His Word and allowing His Spirit lead, guide, and direct them. In doing this, they can take good aim at and emulate His qualities, characteristics, and nature in their own lives. Here are a few targets to aim at:

- Aim at walking by faith not by sight (2 Corinthians 5:7). To walk by faith means to live by what God's Word says, doing what God commands, and thinking like Jesus thinks. Get faith in your sights by practicing what you believe daily.
- Aim at the fruit of the Spirit with its nine bullseyes - love, joy, peace, longsuffering, kindness, goodness, faithfulness, gentleness, and self-control (Galatians 5:22-23). You can develop your skill at doing these nine things by allowing God's Spirit to lead you and practicing them in your life every day.
- Aim at knowing how to pray effectively. Prayer is talking with God. To be skillful and effective in prayer, abide in the Lord and in His Word daily (John 15:7).
- Aim at imitating God by walking in His love, the love that Jesus has for you (Ephesians 5:1-2). God is love, and when He is in your heart you are ready to release His love by loving people like God loves them.

A Christian is someone who follows Jesus, and if you have chosen to follow Him then make sure you have His image in your sight. Let Jesus be the target that you have clearly identified and aim at being just like Him. Reading the Bible every day is like setting up a practice target where you sharpen your shooting skills and practice doing what Jesus said in His Word.

It is God's goal for every Christian to be like Jesus (Romans 8:29-30). Jesus lived like God wants every believer in Him to live. Jesus was determined, submitted, obedient, holy, righteous, loving, kind, uncompromising, led by the Holy Spirit, and everything that a Christian should be. Imitating the way Jesus lived, and knowing how He thought and how He treated people is the best target for your life.

You will find what you need to know about Jesus in the Bible and by His Holy Spirit.

The Word of God is the image of God and Jesus is God's Word made flesh. The Bible gives you an accurate description of what Jesus was like when He walked the earth. It shows you how He interacted with people, how obedient He was to His Father, and how He lived a sinless life. He overcame every challenge He faced, including death by faith. He made it possible for you to follow His example and do what He did with His Holy Spirit helping you all the way. Take good aim at Jesus' life and strive to be like Him.

The apostle Paul was a person who carefully aimed at being like Jesus. He considered his life good for one thing: to finish his race and complete the assignment that Jesus gave him (Acts 20:24). That describes someone who locked onto the target and hit the bullseye. Who do you have in your sights? What have you set your heart on? Take good aim at Jesus and seek to please Him.

When a soldier serves his country, he does not get entangled in civilian pursuits (2 Timothy 2:4). He has one goal and one objective, to follow His commander in chief and obey his orders. For the Christian, Jesus is your Commander in Chief, so make it your aim to please Him. He enlisted you, He rewards you and He gives you the faith to live by. Honor Him by pleasing Him and you will hit the target every time.

Take the time to focus on the ultimate target, Jesus. Hitting the bullseye wins you the ultimate prize, eternal life.

Jesus is the way, the truth and the life. Get a good grip on the truth that Jesus is the only way to God. Aim your heart, like a weapon, at following Jesus Christ and loving Him more than anyone or anything. Take aim at being like Jesus in your thoughts, words, and actions. Look at God's Word, release the safety mechanism on your weapon, squeeze the trigger by taking a leap of faith, and fire at will. You will hit the center of the target, and you will not be disappointed.

CHAPTER 9
THE WALL HANGER – GOING AFTER THE PRIZE

What is the reward for being a Christian? How can I live to get the ultimate prize?

When an outdoorsman goes to hunt or fish, he expects to bring back the biggest game possible, one that is large in size, unique, or beautiful in appearance. He may not bring back a big one every time, but he keeps striving for that goal. He is constantly preparing, practicing, and doing what he loves to do. The prize for his labor, struggle, and effort is to bring home evidence that he accomplished what he set out to do.

When an outdoorsman captures that big game, whatever it may be, his excitement may lead him to put that game on display by mounting it on a wall. This is a way to celebrate and commemorate the occasion. Unless you have a very large home, you would not want to mount any large animals, but you could mount small ones, or parts of ones, like a deer's antlers or hooves. **A wall hanger** is a slang term for an outdoorsman's trophy that hangs on a wall and is a reminder of the challenge it was to catch and kill it.

Mountain climbers have challenging mountains, rocks, or cliffs that they seek to climb. Their wall hanger becomes the ultimate "cliff hanger." They may look for the ultimate peak or try to go higher than anyone has ever gone. Although mountain climbers cannot mount their trophies on their wall, they can mount a selfie of themselves conquering the mountain, rock, or cliff, proving their skillful exploits.

Is there an ultimate prize or wall hanger that a Christian can seek after? Yes, there is. Each person who has surrendered and committed his or her life to follow the Lord Jesus has a prize to gain. The prize for the Christian is not a temporal item like a degree, a natural achievement or an award given to you by some organization. Those are great and should be displayed to demonstrate what you have accomplished, but they are not eternal. The prize for the Christ follower is much greater and goes beyond this natural world. The temporal prizes that can be won are much lower and cannot equal the highest prize which comes only from faithfully following Jesus Christ.

Paul, who wrote about half of the New Testament, described life as a race. Everyone is running in the race but only one receives the prize (1 Corinthians 9:24-27). Don't be discouraged because he said that only one receives the prize. The Scripture encourages you to run in such a way that you may obtain the **prize**. What Paul is saying is that you must run with the same determination and effort that a champion runs with – the determination of someone who will not quit until the race is done. This prize is certainly a great one that will look good hanging on your wall. That means when you reach the end of your life, you will have evidence you lived with a passionate, and obedient pursuit of God, His will, work, and kingdom. What you did for the Lord is what hangs on the wall. Do what God wants you to do.

When you win by running like a champion, God will reward you with an everlasting crown, a crown of life and a home in heaven (1 Corinthians 9:25; James 1:12). You can offer your crowns to Jesus when you get there like the elders do (Revelation 4:4-10). God's prize consists of Jesus saying to you, "Well done, you good and faithful servant: you have been faithful over a few things, I will make you ruler over many things: enter you into the joy of your Lord" (Matthew 25:21). Your prize is the greatest champion, Jesus, greeting, congratulating, and celebrating you as a fellow champion. It is you receiving a kingdom (Luke 22:29). God will reward you as you follow, walk with, and serve Jesus. Do it with all your heart.

The key to winning the heavenly prize is self-control. As you have discovered in earlier pages, hunting and fishing require you to wait, be patient, and exercise self-control when in the outdoors. An outdoorsman must be self-controlled when entering a wooded area, being as quiet as possible while waiting for game to come to him. Also, when an outdoorsman has game in his sights, he must be self-controlled to take careful aim so he can hit the target. A self-controlled hunter and fisherman will gain the prize.

Paul also referenced athletes who exercise self-control to compete for the prize. Have you ever thought about the prizes athletes get? Some of the prizes they can receive are rings, medals, trophies, fame, and money. Think about Olympic athletes who train for years to compete against others from around the world. They must be disciplined in what they eat and how they exercise and train. They must condition their bodies to operate at high levels.

A gold medalist contender is completely dedicated to train to win. People who have won a gold medal believed they could and trained accordingly. To win the ultimate prize as a Christian, you must have a winning mindset. You must see yourself as a winner and be persuaded that you are a winner because Jesus has already won, and He has invited you to be on His winning team. Jesus gives His victory to all who believe in Him, love Him, follow Him, and live like Him.

Paul said another thing about the ultimate prize in

Philippians 3:12-14,

> *"Not that I have already obtained it or have already become perfect, but I press on so that I may lay hold of that for which also I was laid hold of by Christ Jesus. 13 Brethren, I do not regard myself as having laid hold of it yet; but one thing I do: forgetting what lies behind and reaching forward to what lies ahead, 14 I press on toward the goal for the prize of the upward call of God in Christ Jesus."*

He stated that he had not attained it yet nor had he completed his journey. He kept striving for the prize; he pressed on to get a hold of the prize that Christ Jesus promised him. Paul valued God's prize so greatly that he would not quit until he received it. He refused to give up along the way. How can a believer today gain this wall hanger?

The Bible gives us the answer. Philippians 3:13 says to forget those things which are behind. Do not look to your past to reach your destiny. Your destiny is not behind you but in front of you. Secondly, the scripture directs you to reach forward. What are you to reach forward to? You are to reach for Christ Jesus. Keep Him in your sights and stay focused on Jesus. Strive to be just like Him in word, thoughts and deeds. Look to Him for He authored the Bible and will finish all that needs to be done. If Jesus is not in your sights, you will get off track and become lost.

Philippians 3:14 says you should press toward the goal to win. God calls every believer to a high call: to surrender and submit to His will, to live an excellent and abundant life, to be ruled by the law of love, and to spread His good message to everyone you can. That is how you answer God's call. God will reward everyone who follows Jesus wholeheartedly. You cannot lose going after Jesus. Jesus wants you to walk worthy of what He has called you to do.

As you follow Christ you will gain the highest prize: eternal life. Eternal life does not begin when you die; it begins when you accept Jesus as your Lord and Savior. Live like Jesus lived by following His example. **The ultimate prize for the believer - one which he can display on the wall of his life - is a life that reflects Jesus in every area.**

CHAPTER 10
BE AWARE OF YOUR SURROUNDINGS – KNOW THAT GOD LOVES YOU

How can I recognize and know that God loves me? How does God's love help me?

Any time an outdoorsman enters the wilderness he must be aware of his surroundings, especially if he is in an area that he has not been in before. An outdoorsman must possess an awareness to realize, perceive, and know the environment he is in, and what his goal is. He should have a keen eye and good wits, because it is important for him to pay attention to all the details that surround him. His success and safety depend on it.

As an outdoorsman, you must be aware of everything that is around you: trees, plants, animals, different types of terrain, and various conditions like changes in the weather and visibility. Take in the scenery. Ask yourself, what does it look like? Smell like? Feel like? Your surroundings could be life-giving, or dangerous and harmful. Pay attention to what moves around you. Be aware of your feet connecting with the ground, your lungs taking in the air, and the sense of your clothing rubbing against different types of surfaces. When you become aware of your surroundings outside, you harmonize with nature and increase your success in accomplishing your goal.

When you are aware of your surroundings you can

determine the pattern of the area. In other words, you can get a feel of what is going on around you. Every environment has a pattern or a rhythm that includes animal movements, bird and insect calls, and changes in temperature. Become familiar with the pattern of your area.

You may be wondering how being aware of your surroundings relates to following Christ. Just as an atmosphere surrounds an outdoorsman no matter where he travels, there is one main thing that God gives to every person equally and unconditionally on earth: His love. God loved this world so much that He gave His One and only Son, Jesus, and whosoever believes in Him should not perish but have everlasting life (John 3:16). Essentially, God's love surrounds every human being, **though many are not aware that it even exists** and do not know how to work with it or let it work in them.

It is important for anyone in the outdoors to be aware of their surroundings. In the same way, it is also important that both believers and nonbelievers be aware of the love of God that is surrounding them. God's love is everywhere, but you must be able to tap into it to benefit from it. It is this love that draws men to God, forgives them, saves them, and helps them serve others. Love is a very powerful force and an incredible person, namely, God.

As a Christ follower, you need to be aware that God's love exists, is operating, and is ready to do great things. God's love is a powerful force that conquers and casts out fear, covers and releases you from your sin, and leads you to everlasting life. If you are ignorant of the fact that God's love is very near you, you could live your whole life without receiving the rich benefits love offers to you. You could be unaware that love even exists, let alone that it is right there to help you in your darkest hour. If an outdoorsman is unaware of his surroundings, he could die. Learn to discern, recognize, and receive God's love because it will transform your life.

Nelson was again hunting in his friend's blind during archery season. It was a very cold morning and Nelson was having a hard time getting warm. He drank his thermos of hot tea very quickly and he was talking with the Lord about people in Africa that walk great distances to attend church. In a moment he felt as if he was floating up to the tree tops. Nelson had a vision of himself sitting in the blind with Jesus standing beside him with Jesus' arms around him. Jesus' clothes were bright white and brilliant. After this vision, Jesus told Nelson, "It is OK, you can go home." Nelson was so in tune with God's love that it warmed and satisfied him.

When an outdoorsman is aware of his surroundings, he can use that to his advantage. When a Christ follower is aware of God's love surrounding him, he can use that to reach out to others and help them. Jesus told His disciples in Matthew 5:44, "Love your enemies, bless those who curse you, do good to those who hate you, and pray for those who spitefully use you and persecute you." Jesus wanted His disciples to be aware of His love so that they could make a positive impact on the world. You can only love this way by being aware of God's love and letting His love flow through you. If you are unaware of God's love you cannot do what Jesus said to do. Allow God to teach you how to use His love.

You can love the Lord your God with all your being, heart, soul and mind, and you can love your neighbors as yourself, using the love that God surrounds you with (Matthew 22:37-40). Do you wonder who your neighbors are? Your neighbors are everyone you encounter in whatever environment you may be in. They are like the trees, plants, and animals the outdoorsman may encounter in the woods. If you are aware of God's love then you can share with your neighbors who need to experience God's love. God created you, called you, and commanded you to love your neighbor as yourself. Share God's love that He put in your heart with those you see every day.

There are certain things that show up when a person is unaware of their surroundings or do not understand God's love. Jesus told a group of religious leaders in His day that He knew they did not have the love of God in them (John 5:41- 43). How did He know that? The proof that they lacked love was they did not receive Jesus. Jesus is love and when someone rejects Him, they do not have love in them, certainly not God's love. To reject Jesus is to reject God's Word. Many of these leaders could not recognize love in bodily form.

Another proof that many are unaware of their surroundings is they do not think of loving one another as a command. Instead, they view it as an option that they can practice when they feel like it. Jesus identified His true followers as people who have love for one another (John 13:34-35). True disciples of Jesus practice loving others every day. They choose to love people and show their love through their actions. These people are aware of their surroundings.

John 15:12-17 gives further evidence of people who are unaware of their surroundings. People who do not love one another do not serve one another. Love gives sacrificially and lays its life down for others. Serving is a way of laying your life down for others. People who do not love do not obey the Lord's commands. They do not study God's Word, they do not pray, and they probably do not value attending church. These people are not even aware of what God is doing in the earth. They are not connected to God because they are unaware of their surroundings.

The good news is, **if you are unaware of your surroundings - if you are not aware of the reality of the love of God - you can change right now.** You can surrender to God and invite His love into your heart and allow it to work how it wants to work in you. Do not restrict it in any way. His love will come in immediately as you invite Him in, and you will become aware of your surroundings.

CHAPTER 11
BE PREPARED – TAKE THE RIGHT STEPS OF OBEDIENCE

Am I prepared to fully follow Jesus? How can I prepare for eternity?

The Boy Scouts of America is an organization that trains young men to understand, live, and survive in the outdoors. They study plants, animals, and survival skills, and they practice what they learn by going on several camping expeditions throughout the year, even in somewhat harsh conditions. Everything they do enhances their skill to thrive and survive in the outdoors. They have a motto that they stand by which says, "Be prepared." This is a great statement. A boy scout practices being prepared.

As an outdoorsman, you need to be prepared when you enter the wilderness. The wilderness can be unpredictable and you can face many dangers: changes in temperature, unexpected storm fronts that can move in rapidly, and random animal behavior. All these things require you to take extra steps to be prepared.

Hunters need to prepare their weapons, gear, and clothing before arriving at the right hunting spot. The weapons a hunter uses need to be clean, operable, and sighted in to show their range and accuracy before the hunt begins. If the temperature is cold, a hunter needs to dress warm. Hunting may occur on state game lands, which requires the hunter to wear bright reflective clothing that alerts other hunters of his presence. Finally, a hunter needs to have the correct license and know the hunting hours and the limits on how much of each type of game can be taken. Outdoorsmen who hunt need to make many preparations to have a successful and safe hunt.

A fisherman also needs to prepare his gear, clothing, and fishing tools to be able to make a great catch. The first thing he must consider is what kind of pole he should use. This will be determined by what type of fish he is hoping to catch. Secondly, he needs to decide whether he should use live bait or lures to catch the fish. Also, he needs to decide if he will be fishing from a boat, the shore, or a dock. Another thing he needs to consider is if he should bring rain gear. Different settings may require different shoes or additional equipment. Good fishermen take the time to prepare for what is known and even what is unknown. Every outdoorsman needs to be prepared when entering the outdoors.

What does it mean for the Christ follower to be prepared? Being prepared means being ready to obey everything that Jesus commands you to do: to go where He says go, and to be what He tells you to be. A Christian's preparation is taking the right steps of obedience daily. Ultimately, every Christian is preparing for Jesus to return to establish His kingdom forever. Even though this has not yet occurred, until it does, a Christian should live every day hearing, believing, and doing God's will faithfully by obeying what He says. Any step that you take in obedience to the Lord Jesus Christ is a right step that prepares you to be ready for His return.

God leads His followers in steps. The Bible says, "**The steps** of a good man are ordered by the Lord and He delights in his way" (Psalms 37:23-24). In the book of Psalms it says,

"God directs believer's steps by His Word" (Psalms 119:133). If they saw all that God planned for them to do, they wouldn't be able to handle it all at once.

When I asked God what he wanted me to do in my life, He gave me the name of a Bible school, Rhema Bible Training Center, in Tulsa OK. He wanted me to attend that school. He didn't say anything else about what He wanted until I sent in my application. He showed me what step to take, I took it, and He spoke again. He led me step-by-step into His perfect will for my life.

God also leads His followers in steps because steps require faith. When God shows you a step to take, you must act by faith and take that step in order to see the next step. Every step you take requires you to stop and listen to God's voice so He can tell you the next step. Every step you take must be coordinated with what God says.

If an outdoorsman enters the wilderness unprepared, he could be overwhelmed, harmed, and unsuccessful in attaining his goal. Also, a Christian who is unprepared when Jesus returns could miss out on great benefits that he would have received if he was prepared.
A Christian must stay prepared every day.

Jesus told a parable in Matthew 25 that explains why a Christian should be prepared. The main characters in this parable are ten virgins who carry oil lamps as they wait to meet the bridegroom, who represents Christ. Five of the virgins are wise and five are foolish. To be unprepared is foolishness. The five foolish ones brought lamps but no extra oil. The five wise ones took their lamps along with extra oil.

A cry was heard at midnight saying, "The bridegroom is coming, go meet him" (Matthew 25:6). The foolish virgins ran out of oil and asked the wise ones to give them some oil. The wise refused, telling their foolish companions to go and buy their own oil. While the foolish virgins were away looking for oil, they missed seeing the bridegroom and were disqualified from enjoying his presence, all because they were not prepared. The Lord said that he did not even know them. Wow! Because they were not prepared, they missed the greatest opportunity of their life. When you do not take steps of obedience daily, you miss things that God has prepared for you.

God led my friend Nelson to a different church and for his obedience God brought three major blessings to him in a short period of time: a new job, a newer vehicle, and a wife! If he had disobeyed, he would have missed those good things. I also took several steps of obedience to become the pastor of Victory Christian Fellowship. If I had failed to obey, I would have missed out on what God had for me. Be prepared and follow the steps the Lord leads you to take.

Just as an outdoorsman is successful in the outdoors when he is prepared, a Christian is successful as he or she continues obeying whatever God says. Obedience is hearing what God says, trusting what He says, and doing it. You can train yourself to hear God's voice. Disobedience mistrusts the Lord, does not carry out His command, and opens the door for God to judge you accordingly. God is more pleased when His followers obey Him than when His followers sacrifice something for God's cause (1 Samuel 15:22-23). Jesus showed us how to be obedient through His example. Jesus obeyed everything His Father commanded Him so you could receive grace, righteousness and life. Be determined to obey God your whole life, and you will always be ready to participate in God's great plan.

CHAPTER 12
WALKING THROUGH THE DARKNESS – ALLOW THE LIGHT TO LEAD YOU

Is there a way to move through the darkness that is in this world?

Every outdoorsman needs access to a light to help him navigate through the darkness of the wilderness. **Darkness is temporary but light is eternal.** God has given this world the greatest light to bring everyone who believes in Him out of darkness. Believe in God's light, receive His light and walk in His light, and you will be free of the darkness.

Many outdoor activities can be carried out in the day or at night. If you are outdoors at nighttime, you must deal with the darkness. The darkness can be challenging and dangerous. It makes movement slow and difficult, things are not easily recognized when there is no light, rough terrain that could cause injury is hidden by darkness, and several animal predators hunt at night. There is one simple tool that you can use to move through darkness: light. Light is powerful, portable, adjustable, and makes darkness flee. As a Christ follower, you must learn to be led by the light.

Here are some reasons why darkness is challenging and dangerous in both the outdoor world and the spiritual world.

- **Darkness is light deficient. Darkness will remain until it is met by light, then it will scatter.**

- Darkness is a good concealer. Many things, both good and bad, can hide in darkness.
- Darkness obscures things so you can easily recognize what they are. It causes targets to be unclear so they cannot be hit.
- Darkness is never associated with things good, but things wicked, evil and sinister.
- Darkness is associated with immorality. Immoral acts are by people whose hearts are dark.
- Darkness is linked to ignorance. A darkened mind is one that is unable to discern between right and wrong.

Here are a few ways how light can be helpful to an outdoorsman. A night fisherman needs light to prepare tackle, bait a hook, and identify what is caught. Light is required to spot the game that is hunted at night. Without light, a hunter could not see or hit his target. Campers make a fire for light, warmth and protection. Even the military uses night vision goggles which enhance their ability to see in darkness. **Light unveils what the darkness hides. You can only dispel darkness with light.**

A successful outdoorsman needs to be able to navigate through the darkness. There are times you may move through the wilderness in darkness to get to your hunting spot. If you do this without the help of a light, it could be hazardous to you. You could miss what is hidden in the darkness and cause injury to yourself. If you do not have a light, you can still move in darkness, but your movement is slow, cautious and methodical. The light makes things that were difficult easier. If you must move through dark areas, use a light to guide your way.

Just like an outdoorsman can use a light to navigate

through darkness, God has also provided His followers with light to make their way through darkness. God knows that this world is full of darkness, and He wants to bring you out of it and into His light. "God is light" (1 John 1:5). Jesus said, "I have come as a light into the world, that whoever believes in Me should not abide in darkness" (John 12:46-47). It is only by following the light that you can overcome darkness.

When God created this world, the earth was empty, a formless mass cloaked in darkness according to the New Living Translation of Genesis 1:2. God then created light by saying, "Let there be light," and there was light. He did not want you to be in darkness, so the first thing He made was light. The light that God made was good. Our Father God never described darkness as good.

Darkness is associated with negative things.

- The devil who is the adversary of Christianity, has a branch of his army called "rulers of darkness of this age" (Ephesians 6:12).
- Jesus described your eye as the lamp of your body and He said, "If your eye is bad, your whole body will be full of darkness" (Matthew 6:22-23). He described darkness as something bad.
- The Bible calls darkness "unfruitful" (Ephesians 5:11).
- Any person who has failed to accept Christ as their Savior before they die will be "cast into darkness where there is weeping and teeth grinding" (Matthew22:13).

The light of the Lord helps you overcome all the negative effects of darkness. A light is good for an outdoorsman and it is good for a Christian too.

Light changes the atmosphere of darkness and makes darkness flee. Psalms 112:4 tells us that a light arises in darkness for the upright. One who is upright is right with God and living the way God wants him to live. It is interesting that this verse declares that light arises in darkness. If an outdoorsman is making his way to a stand in darkness, he may use a flashlight that arises in the darkness to light his way and help him arrive safely. God has a light to counteract and overcome any darkness you may experience.

God has given you light to help you navigate through any darkness and dark times that you may encounter in life. **God never designed darkness to be permanent.** The Lord Jesus is the Light of the World (John 8:12). If you are walking in the dark and feel like there is no light to help you, the prophet Isaiah has an encouraging word for you: you can trust in the name of the Lord and rely on Him (Isaiah 50:9-10). God is the light you need to bring you out of darkness. Also, His Word is a lamp to your feet and a light to your path (Psalms 119:105).

Zechariah, father of John the Baptist, prophesied about his son and his purpose in life. He declared that part of John's ministry was to give light to those who sat in darkness and the shadow of death (Luke 1:79). This light would guide them into the way of peace. The Lord Jesus did something great for all who sit in darkness. He gave them light that brought them out of darkness. Just as an outdoorsman uses light to move through the darkness, a Christian uses light to change negative circumstances into positive ones.

Light is powerful and a bright light can be blinding to the human eye. Light is measured in lumens. A lumen measures the total amount of visible light from the beam or angle originating from the light source. The more lumens a light has the brighter it shines. Just as light can increase in lumens, so can a believer increase in brightness. The Bible reveals that the righteous person's path can progressively become brighter (Proverbs 4:18). The level of brightness you need depends on how much darkness you need to dispel.

Just as man-made lights can be powerful, God's light is much more powerful. The apostle Paul described encountering a light in the middle of the day that was "brighter than the sun" (Acts 26:13). Jesus revealed His glory to a few of his disciples and "His face shone like the sun, and His clothes became white as the light" (Matthew 17:2-3). God's light is so bright that it will illuminate His city (Revelation 21:23-24).

The life of God actually gives light to everyone. When you receive the Lord in your heart, He gives you light, illuminates you within, and changes your life. **His light is so powerful that it shines through darkness, and the darkness can never extinguish it** (John 1:3-5). The light of Jesus will shine forever, never dimming or fading or going out. Once you encounter the light of Jesus you will never want to return to the darkness.

The light of God has come to all mankind. Jesus is the light of God. But not all men like the light or are drawn to it. Some people love darkness more than the light because they are evil (John 3:19-21). A person who practices evil hates the light and does not come to the light. The light of Jesus is the truth, so if you want to come out of the darkness then follow the truth and apply your life to it. **Deciding to do the truth is just like turning on a light in the wilderness and allowing that light to guide your path.** When a light guides you, it does not illuminate the entire area, but it shines enough to show you where to walk and where not to walk. Stay on the path that the light makes.

An outdoorsman has only two options when moving through the darkness. Allow a light to lead him or let the darkness overtake him. A Christ follower has the light and must believe in it to become a child of God (John 12:35-36). There is only one light that will lead you through darkness, give you true eternal life and help you to succeed in life: the light of God, Jesus Christ.

God will never leave an outdoorsman, who believes in Jesus Christ, stranded in darkness. The Lord desires to open people's eyes, and to turn them from darkness to light, and from the power of Satan to God (Acts 26:17-18). **Satan's power works in darkness. Jesus is light. Jesus shines in the darkness, exposes what the darkness is doing, and brings you out of it.** God forgives you for what you did while you were in darkness and He gives you an inheritance so you can have a better more abundant life. God actually calls you out of darkness and invites you to come into His marvelous light.

If you have encountered the light of God and made Jesus your Lord and Savior, then change the way you live. Walking in the light means living like Christ Jesus lived while He was on earth and continues to live in heaven (1 John 1:6-7). You must put away the works of darkness and stop doing what you did when you had no light (Romans 13:12-13). Just follow the light for it will guide your steps.

In order for you to navigate through the darkness in this world, you need the light of Jesus Christ to shine in you and on your path. Choose to allow the light of God to help you go through and overcome the darkness.

CHAPTER 13
THE BAIT – RESIST TEMPTATION AND AVOID BEING HOOKED

How can I overcome temptation?

Bait is what outdoorsmen use to lure and attract prey. It is usually something that is appealing to a prey and it catches its eye. Bait is used by fishermen, hunters, and trappers, and it is designed to draw prey into a location where a predator may be waiting. Bait can draw prey to or into captivity or its doom.

Satan uses bait also, called temptation. With it, he tries to draw mankind away from God, church, right family relationships, and respect of authority. The temptation that the devil uses affects mankind in three areas of the world: sinful cravings, the lust of the eyes, and the boasting of what man has and what he does, (1 John 2:15-16 NIV). It is only through a relationship with Jesus Christ and knowing His Word that you can resist and overcome temptation.

It is the desire of Satan to steal, kill, destroy, and take you captive for eternity. Taking Satan's bait allows him to put his hooks in you to ensnare and enslave you. He does this through deception, manipulation, accusation, and temptation. He is a bondage-maker but Christ is the bondage-breaker. Although the devil cannot make you do anything, he presents you with thoughts, ideas, and suggestions that contradict

God's Word. If you allow thoughts that contradict God's Word to reside in your mind, you will act on those thoughts, taking the bait of Satan, and you will be trapped by him.

Nelson's Bible Dictionary defines temptation as "an enticement or invitation to sin, with the implied promise of greater good to be derived from following the way of disobedience." Generally understood, temptation is when sin appears to be advantageous, even good. It is enticing. Temptation may appeal to your feelings, but, beware! It is a trap.

Temptation is deceptive, infectious, and seductive, and it leads to ultimate destruction, hell. The bait of your enemy is designed to trap you so he can steal, kill, and destroy you. The devil is skilled in the art of deception, being a master deceiver. He uses the force of fear and intimidation to get you to comply with his plan to destroy you. He threatens you with violence and harm. He arouses fleshly desires (lust of flesh and eyes, and the pride of life) and seduces you to divulge your secrets. Don't take the devil's bait because it leads to destruction.

God does not tempt anyone, nor can He be tempted by evil. People are tempted through their own fleshly desires. A conceived desire becomes sin which leads to death (James 1:13-15). There is one tempter, the devil, and he manipulates your weaknesses and tempts you where you lack self-control. The good news is he can be resisted with the Word of God, (Matthew 4:1-3; 1 Corinthians 7:5).

Ways to Overcome Temptation

You can avoid taking Satan's bait and overcome any temptation that you face. God has equipped you with all you need to resist the enemy and defeat him. Here are some tools that will help you not become Satan's prey.

Prayer – Prayer is a powerful weapon that you can use to resist temptation. Bait is simply an offer that can be refused. Pray when you start your day to not be led into temptation and to be delivered from the evil one (Matthew 6:13; Luke 22:40).

Stay alert, watch, pray – In your darkest hour, stop what you are doing, drop to your knees, and pray to God in the name of Jesus. Jesus' disciples could not pray for one hour (Mark 14:37-38). Prayer could have given them divine strength.

God makes a way out for you – He always has a way out for you to move away from temptation (1 Corinthians 10:13 NLT). Take the way out that He provided for you.

- God provides you with other tools to help you be victorious over temptation. His presence covers you, His mercy holds you up if you slip, and He comforts your anxieties (Psalm 94:17-19).
- God's Word helps you to avoid Satan's snares (Psalms 119:110).
- Jesus used God's Word when He said, "It is written" (Luke 4).
- Jesus was tempted just like we are, yet without sin, and He is able to aid those who are tempted (Hebrews 2:18). Ask Him to help you (Hebrews 4:15-16

Godliness is a defense against temptation – Godliness does what is right and overcomes temptation. It avoids being dominated by the tendencies of your flesh, and helps you to be clean, holy, and pure. It honors God's authority and submits to His Lordship (2 Peter 2:8-11).

Choose the Right Path – You decide what path to take, the wicked way or the right path. Do not let the devil lead you into wickedness or evil (Proverbs 4:14-15).

Resist – The gospel of Jesus Christ directs man to resist temptation, promising blessing to those who do. Victorious faith overcomes temptation and gives you a crown of life, (James 1:12; 1 John 5:4). You can refuse Satan's bait in Christ. Make this statement, "I resist temptation in Jesus' name."

Be full of God's Spirit – Jesus was filled with the Spirit, underwent severe temptation for forty days, and came out more powerful because He refused the bait (Luke 4:1-14). Being filled with God's Spirit gives you an advantage over the enemy.

Overcome Sexual Temptation – You can avoid the sexual temptation bait. Joseph refused the advances of his master's wife (Genesis 29:8-10). You can live according to a higher standard.

Do not Consent – If sinners entice you, do not consent. Say No (Proverbs 1:10). You do not have to give into peer pressure. Stand up for what is right.

Faith – Faith is a shield that quenches the enemy's fiery darts and stops what your enemy hurls at you (Ephesians 6:15-16). You can resist the enemy and his bait by faith (1 Peter 5:8-10).

A Spirit of Gentleness – Gentleness protects you from temptation like raingear protects your body from moisture. Spiritual men are gentle but not weak because they restore a fallen brother being aware of their own frailty (Galatians 6:1).

Maintain a Tender Heart – Rocky soil describes a person with a hard heart. A hard-hearted person has no roots in God, so when offered Satan's bait, that person falls away. A tender-hearted person receives and cherishes God's Word, and is established in Him deeply (Luke 8:13-14). Maintain a tender heart by taking responsibility for your mistakes and continually get up to move forward.

Do Not Love Money – Money is a tool but it was never meant to rule. A desire to get rich quick can be a snare of temptation. Love God more than money and He will meet your needs according to His riches and glory in Christ (1 Timothy 6:9-10).

Do Not Love the World – Do not love the sinful elements of human life that operate in the world's system, those immoral tendencies and pursuits which give the world its evil character. Make God your first love and you can resist the bait of Satan (1 John 2:15-16)

Know Satan is the Tempter – Satan was the one who influenced Judas to betray Jesus (John 13:2). Satan will try to influence you, but you can resist him. The Bible shows you what Satan does so you can resist his tricks.

Satan's bait, temptation, is designed to snare, trap and capture you so he can destroy you. You can avoid the bait altogether by using these tools that God has given to you. As you grow in your relationship with God, you will become more skilled in avoiding the bait of Satan.

CHAPTER 14
FROM THE STRIKE ZONE – TO THE FAITH ZONE

How can I express my faith? What does it mean to act in faith?

When an outdoorsman takes the necessary steps to prepare, to set up, to wait alert and ready, and to look diligently for the right moment to achieve his goal, then he strikes. The strike is the instant that will determine if the outdoorsman comes home with a prize or leaves empty-handed. In a moment's notice he must be quick to act, whether that be to catch, bag, or capture prey.

The strike is the moment that makes the difference for the fisherman and hunter. It is the moment when an outdoorsman must act and strike the target to turn the prey into his prize. A fisherman waits for the moment when the fish has seized the bait. As soon as the pole vibrates and begins to bend, the fisherman makes his strike by jerking his pole upward to set the line. The action taken with his pole hooks a fish so it can be reeled in. In hunting, the strike is the action a hunter takes in aiming and firing at a target. The strike is the sudden action that that turns the target into your trophy.

The strike happens in a small window of opportunity and has a limited range. A hunter may only have a moment where he can hit a target that is clear, within range, and still long enough for him to strike. Many outdoorsmen have failed in achieving their goal because they miss opportunities that were available to them. When you see your opportunity, you must act immediately.

Fish themselves have strike zones. Understanding strike zones of fish has a huge effect on the fisherman's success. The strike zone of a fish is the distance wherein a fish has a high probability of capturing prey. If you are fishing with a lure, you must place that lure within the strike zone of the fish. A fish will probably not go after prey that is not in its strike zone. A fisherman must make precise casts, in the strike zone, and retrieve those casts skillfully to catch the big one. People who do much bass fishing with lures may cast and reel many times while fishing. It takes patience, diligence, and skill to cast multiple times in a few hours. Sometimes it may be the twentieth or thirtieth cast that puts your hook in the zone of a big one.

The distance an animal can attack prey varies greatly between species. Carnivores in the animal kingdom, are limited to moments of opportunities and the range in which they can attack. If a prey comes within a predator's range, the predator has high probability of capturing that prey. If a prey exceeds the range of a predator, it has a greater chance to escape. Sometimes a predator misses its prey because it failed to get it even though it was within range. A failure to strike within range and at the right moment leaves predators hungry. Knowing when to strike and how to strike is important for survival.

You now know that a strike in the outdoors is seizing an opportunity and acting on it. So, how would a Christ follower define a strike? For the Christian, **the strike is taking a step of faith and acting on God's Word when it is heard.** The moment you hear the Word of God on any subject, it is within your range and you must act on it to possess what it says – you hear it, believe it, act on it and receive it. The believer's strike zone is the faith zone. The faith zone is where you act and respond to what God said. Your action is a catalyst that activates God's power to manifest His words into reality.

A Christian actively goes after God's promises. When a Christ follower believes God's Word and puts it into action, power is released to make God's Word a reality in his life. God's Word is true and it is forever settled in heaven. It does not need to be changed or altered; it is complete as it is. All you need to do is put your trust in God's Word and do what it says.

Whether you believe God's Word or not, His Word remains true and powerful forever. But if you want God's Word to change your life, you must believe it and act on it. Believing God's Word is receiving it and benefit from what it says. The Bible only benefits those who trust in it wholeheartedly, carry out its commands diligently, and practice its principles faithfully.

According to James 1:22-25, hearing God's Word is not enough; you must do what it says so you can reap the benefits that are associated with it. If there is no action taken on God's Word there are no rewards received. James also says in verse 25, "That those who do what the Bible says are blessed in what they do." The action you take in believing and obeying God's Word makes the difference in your life.

Operating in faith is very simple. Many years ago, I learned an important principle of how faith works from cutting grass. I finished mowing a lawn and was weeding the lawn with an electric weed eater. The bottom of the weed eater where the cutting string was contained became loose and flew off the trimmer while it was spinning. The piece that flew off was green, the same color as the grass. I wondered how I was going to find a small green circular piece of plastic in a sea of green. I had a window of opportunity to act. I prayed and asked God to help me find the missing piece so I could finish my job. After I prayed, I walked around that yard, thanking God for showing me where the piece was. If you had seen me, you may have thought that I was acting crazy, but I seriously trusted God to help me. I had faith, and I acted on it. After about twenty-five minutes, I stopped, looked across the yard and under a bush, and there I saw the missing piece. I fixed the trimmer and finished the job. Faith works when you work it.

Hebrews chapter 11 is dedicated to people who entered the faith zone. It has been described as the "Hall of Faith" because it highlights the great exploits and accomplishments of many different people who acted on what God said when they heard Him speak. People in this chapter are biblical action heroes who took their window of opportunity and did what God said. Upon hearing what God said and seeing what He promised, these people acted quickly to do what God said and to claim His promises. We are going to look at a few examples of people who entered the faith zone.

Hebrews 11:1 says, "Now faith is the substance of things hoped for, the evidence of things not seen." God's holy Word is the only evidence that you need to prove something exists. When you know what God has promised you, from hearing His word and allowing His Word to enter your heart, you have entered the strike zone and you can receive what He said. The moment you believe that you have received what God said is the moment you hit your target like an outdoorsman hits his mark. Go after what God has spoken and written with your entire being.

The Amplified Bible expands this verse saying, "NOW FAITH is the assurance (the confirmation, the title deed) of the things [we] hope for, being the proof of things [we] do not see and the conviction of their reality [faith perceiving as real fact what is not revealed to the senses]" (Hebrews 11:1 AMP).

Whatever God asks you to do requires you to step out in faith. To be strong in faith is to do what God says in the Bible - you must be assured of who God is, what He said was true, and that it cannot fail. Christ followers know that God cannot lie because the closer they walk with Him, the better they know Him and become more confident in His Word. When He speaks, they can simply do what He said.

Hebrews 11:5-6 tells of a man named Enoch that was taken to heaven because he pleased God. Simply pleasing God was the action that Enoch took in the faith zone. Did you know that it takes faith to please God? Pleasing God requires you to have a relationship with Him - by having Him in your sights, going after Him with all your heart, and doing what He says the moment He speaks. Pleasing God takes faith. You must believe that God exists and that He rewards those who faithfully follow Him. Enter the faith zone, set your sights on God, and pursue Him with your whole being.

Another person who entered the faith zone was Noah (Hebrews 11:7 God spoke to Noah and commanded him to build a giant boat to save humanity. Noah knew when he heard God's Word that it was the moment to act. God warned Noah of things not yet seen, and **Noah moved with godly fear** and prepared an ark. Can you imagine preparing for rain preparing for rain not knowing what it was or have ever seeing it? That is entering the faith zone. Genesis 2:5-6 says, "For the LORD God **had not caused it to rain on the earth,** and there was no man to till the ground; 6 but **a mist went up from the earth and watered the whole face of the ground."**

According to Hebrews 11:7 Noah performed these actions

in the faith zone

- He moved with reverence for God by immediately obeying God's instructions.
- He prepared an ark. The ark was a massive building project that took many years to complete. Noah went after that task wholeheartedly. He was compelled to obey God by doing what He said. He resisted criticism, antagonism, and the pure evil that surrounded him, remaining undaunted in his task. He seized God's promise like a fisherman sets his line. Noah hooked on doing God's will. Make it your aim to go after God like Noah did.
- He saved his household. The action he took resulted in his family being rescued from the flood. The actions you take when God speaks are very important.

A final example we want to share with you is Abraham. Abraham entered the faith zone when he set his sights on his inheritance. In Genesis 12:1-3 God told Abraham to leave his country, family and his father's house. God wanted Abraham to move in a direction, but didn't reveal to him the final destination. As Abraham stepped in faith, God would tell him where to go. Abraham's reward for his obedience was four-fold: he would become a great nation, he would be blessed, his name would be great, and Abraham would bless others also. Genesis 12:4 shows us how Abraham responded to this opportunity, "He departed as the Lord had spoken to him." He entered the faith zone and took advantage of his opportunity.

Hebrews 11:8-10 describes the actions that Abraham took as **he obeyed, he went out and he dwelt where God showed him.** The faith zone is when any believer sets their sights on what God says and goes after it enthusiastically and faithfully. The Word of God is the target of all who believe. If you want what God says to happen in your life, you must do what He says. Your faith always moves forward and upward. Faith makes you move because you have God in your sights.

Your faith requires action just like fishing or hunting requires action if there are to be any results. Fishermen must set their hooks and reel in fish; hunters must aim and pull the trigger to hit their target animal. So to, you must act on God's Word to take hold of what He has promised you. Enter your faith zone today and do what God says when He says it.

CHAPTER 15
THE RIGHT WEAPON AND THE RIGHT AMMO – SPEAKING GOD'S WORD.

Does speaking God's Word improve my life? How can I defeat the devil?

If you are an outdoorsman who loves to hunt, you know that different hunts require different weapons. Some hunters are more skilled in using certain weapons than others. There are weapons that are very versatile and can be used on many different hunts. Each weapon you may use requires a different skill set. Throughout history, mankind has used a variety of weapons to hunt. When you hunt, use the weapon you are most skilled with to give you the greatest success in your pursuit. For our purposes, we will focus on three different weapons: the shotgun, the rifle, and the bow.

Since there are so many weapons to choose from, know that different weapons use different ammunition. For example, when hunting waterfowl like ducks and geese, the weapon of choice is a shotgun that uses shells. Shotguns come in different gauges that measure the power of the gun, ranging from eight to twenty, depending on what the gun will be used for.

A shotgun shell is a plastic case that contains BB's, small round metal balls. It is designed with a brass bottom containing the gunpowder that is needed to propel the BB's through the barrel of the gun. A shotgun shell launches out in a wider pattern than a bullet. The wider pattern makes hunting waterfowl much easier. Shotguns normally hold three shells at a time and can be semi-automatic or pump action. A semi-automatic gun places the ammo in the chamber automatically and allows a hunter to simply pull the trigger to fire the weapon. It can fire three shots very quickly. A pump action gun requires a hunter to pump the gun after each shot, so that he can put a shell in the chamber. If you use a shotgun, then you know that you will need shotgun shells.

Hunters who hunt bigger game need to use a rifle. In comparison to a shotgun, a rifle has a long barrel with spiral grooves inside to make the bullet spin. This design improves the accuracy over a long distance. Rifles can hit targets at a much longer distance than shotguns. A scope can even be mounted on a rifle to view targets that are a great distance away. As a rifle increase in power, so its ammo increases in size. An outdoorsman needs greater skill to aim at a target with a rifle verses a shotgun.

Bullets are made out of several metals. They contain gunpowder inside, and when a bullet is struck on the bottom, the projectile is launched. Magazines are containers that hold several bullets the rifle can fire. Being able to fire more rounds than a shotgun gives hunters an advantage. Hunters use rifles in places that have vast open areas because bullets can easily travel two miles or more.

A bow is an incredible and versatile tool to use outdoors because it can be used for both hunting and fishing. It brings the two sports together. Bow fishing uses barbed arrows attached to the bow with a string to retrieve fish that are caught.

A bow is a simple weapon that has existed for many

centuries. Many bows do not have sights, unlike their compound counterparts, and aiming is by line-of-sight judgment down the arrow. There are three main types of bows: long, recurve, and compound bows. There are also bows called crossbows that are similar to rifles.

The arrows that are used in bow fishing are considerably heavier and stronger that arrows used in other types of archery. Arrows for fishing are commonly constructed of fiberglass, solid aluminum, carbon fiber, or carbon fiber reinforced fiberglass. These arrows do not have the feathers at the end so they can go through water better.

An outdoorsman can use a bow for a wide variety of prey. A bow can take down big prey like bear, elk or deer, and small prey like fish. It may take more than one arrow to take down bigger prey. A hunter usually carries a quiver that contains several arrows on his back, at his side, or on the bow itself. A highly skilled bowman may shoot more than one arrow at the same time, but most archers shoot one arrow at a time.

Up until this point, we have described different weapons, the ammunition they require, and different ways to use the weapons. What types of weapons and ammunition does a Christian use? Christians have an array of weapons to choose from like the name of Jesus, God's Word, praise and prayer, and the Holy Spirit. The main weapon a Christ follower uses is their mouth. The ammunition that comes out of the mouth should be the Word of God.

1Timothy 6:12 describes how believers should fight. It mentions that profession is part of fighting the good fight. Profession has to do with your mouth. Your mouth is your spiritual shotgun, rifle, and bow. Your heart is the chamber that holds your ammo that is ready to be launched out of your mouth. Scriptures from the Bible are the only effective ammo that will stop your enemy in his tracks.

A great example of how a person's mouth was a weapon is found in the story of David verses Goliath in 1 Samuel 17. One man, named Goliath, spoke words against Israel for forty days. Using intimidating words, fear-filled words, and belittling words, one man caused the entire army of Israel to be afraid. "When Saul and all Israel heard these words of the Philistine, they were dismayed and greatly afraid" (1 Samuel 17:11). Here you can see that someone armed with negative words can potentially paralyze an army.

David came on the scene to confront Goliath. Before there was any physical combat, the battle of the words had to be won. You will see who had a more superior weapon, better ammunition, and a more accurate aim to hit the target. David was the predator and Goliath was the trophy prey that was about to suffer defeat.

The battle begins in verse 43. Goliath launched the first strike against David by attempting to make fun of David's choice of weapon, sticks. David went to face Goliath with a staff in his hand. Goliath did not think that David was a worthy opponent, so Goliath cursed David. The giant that opposed David taunted him and tried to intimidate him by saying that he would give his flesh to the birds and the beasts.

Now it was David's turn to go on the attack and launch his real weapon. David was not intimidated by the giant's words. He had superior ammunition to launch from his own mouth. In verse 45-47, David declared boldly that he was coming against Goliath with the name of the Lord of Hosts, the God of the armies of Israel. This clearly places the battle on a spiritual plane. He recognized that Goliath's words were really against God. David, realizing that the Lord's own power was the gunpowder in his ammo, proclaimed that Goliath would be struck dead and decapitated. With extreme confidence, he declared that the battle was the Lord's.

It turns out that what David said was correct. His weapon and ammo was superior to his opponent's. Goliath lost and David did exactly what he said he was going to do. He won the battle of the words and he won the physical battle too. A fierce, giant warrior was defeated by someone smaller in stature, lesser in strength, and not as experienced in combat. David's words won and his actions completed his sentence.

Just as an outdoorsman can use different weapons for different activities, believers in Christ Jesus possess a supreme weapon their mouth with which they can speak God's Word, their ammo, to gain victories and stop prey in their tracks. You must become skilled at speaking God's Word with your own mouth to get the results that David did.

CHAPTER 16
KEEP YOUR WEAPON CLEAN – RENEW YOUR MIND

Does renewing my mind really change my life? Can I really live a clean life?

It is one thing to have the right weapon and ammo for what you are hunting for. It is another thing to maintain your weapon to make sure it is always in good working order. Every activity an outdoorsman is engaged in requires him to have working tools that are up for the task in which he uses them. It would be bad for a hunter to have his weapon misfire because it was poorly maintained, especially if he had a prize game in his sights! It would not be good for a fisherman to try to cast his line in a hot spot where the fish are biting and have his line get tangled in his reel due to lack of maintenance. An outdoorsman must be able to maintain the tools of his trade.

Hunters must clean their guns and weapons to make sure they continually work well for a very long time. Guns are designed to be taken apart so they can be cleaned and oiled easily. This keeps your weapon in good working order, preventing misfires and prolonging its life and usefulness. Keeping your outdoor tools maintained is just as important as maintaining a vehicle regularly. Unmaintained equipment wears down more quickly, rusts, and eventually becomes useless.

Keeping your weapon clean gives you confidence knowing that it will work when you need it to work. The military trains its soldiers to take apart and put together their weapons, even blindfolded, so they can do it in all environments. Weapon maintenance is a part of hunting that may not be the most fun, but it is necessary. Doing these little things regularly make a big difference in the success of the hunt.

If an outdoorsman has to regularly maintain his weapon to make it work well, what does a Christ follower have to maintain? A Christ follower has to maintain the renewing of his mind on a regular basis. A Christian who renews his mind is like an outdoorsman who cleans his weapon.

Renewing your mind is a way to be cleansed of the world. Living in the world every day is like hunting and fishing in the wilderness. In both the world and the wilderness you get filthy, dirty, and you start to stink. Upon leaving the outdoors after hunting or fishing, an outdoorsman will need to bathe. Upon choosing Christ above the way of world, a Christian's mind will need to be bathed, or be renewed. Renewing your mind is the key to operating in God's kingdom successfully. It cleanses the filth, dirt, and stench from your mind that it picked up in the world. Just like an unmaintained weapon could malfunction, a mind that is not renewed could hinder a believer from living for Christ effectively and receiving the benefits Christ offers.

Romans 12:1-2 tells you how to renew your mind. There are several parts involved in renewing your mind:

- Step one - Renewing your mind involves presenting your body as a living sacrifice. When you choose to follow Christ, you must bring your body under a new set of principles with higher standards, and a new way of living. Offer your body to the Lord as a clean instrument, in good working order, so you can serve God diligently.

Your mind controls your body just like a hunter controls his gun. Before a hunt, a hunter checks his gun, making sure it is in good working order, and all the moving parts are operating as they should. Before coming to Christ, you thought differently about the world, people, and God. When you accept Jesus as your Lord, your body must be trained to live like Jesus wants you to live and not the way you used to live. As you renew your mind, you no longer do things that are evil, wicked, wrong, or against the Lord, but you begin to do things that please God, and are right and pure according to His Holy Word. You put your body in good working order and present it to Christ. Renewing your mind helps you to transform your body into a powerful weapon that Christ can use for His divine purposes and plans.

- Step two - Renewing your mind helps you to become holy. Peter, an apostle of Jesus, wrote, "Therefore gird up the loins of your mind, be sober, and rest your hope fully upon the grace that is to be brought to you at the revelation of Jesus Christ; 14 as obedient children, not conforming yourselves to the former lusts, as in your ignorance; 15 but as He who called you is holy, you also be holy in all your conduct, 16 because it is written, 'Be holy, for I am holy'" (1 Peter 1:13-16).

Peter talked about your mind and how you can renew it. Part of renewing your mind is exercising self-control. This Scripture, in 1 Peter 1, encourages you to rest your hope fully upon the grace that came when you met Christ. It also admonishes you not to be conformed to your former lusts, those things you desired in the world without Christ in your heart. Finally, it tells you to be holy, just as the Lord is holy. Holiness comes through following Jesus' example. Continue to read about His life in the Bible so you can act like Him.

The word "holy" also means "clean." When an outdoorsman cleans his weapon, he wipes it down, takes it apart, and cleans the barrel of the gun inside and out. When Jesus comes into your life, He wipes you down with His blood and begins to clean you from the inside out. Renewing your mind is a daily duty of everyone who believes in Jesus Christ as Lord and it is how you maintain your life in Christ, continually being useful to Him.

> • Step three - Renewing your mind according to this passage in Romans 12, results in a life acceptable to God. The Bible is very clear about what God accepts and rejects. Renewing your mind means you begin to think, speak, and act like Jesus. You do what God wants, you love what He loves, you hate what He hates, and you put Him first in all things. Whatever your goal was before you met Christ shifts to make the goal of pleasing God your highest priority. A renewed mind is acceptable to God like a clean weapon is acceptable to an outdoorsman.

> • Step four - Renewing your mind is when you discover what God's will is for your life. God created and designed you to be like Jesus, just like every gun maker designed their guns to shoot. Before you were born, God created you with a divine purpose and plan. Renewing your mind helps you to focus on pleasing God and increases your ability to understand why you were

created.

As you read the Bible, you will discover how God's kingdom works, so you can become more like Jesus and you can set a course to please God for the rest of your life. Perform daily maintenance by renewing your mind so that you will be an instrument acceptable to God and ready for every good work (2 Tim 2:21).

CHAPTER 17
CLEAN THE GAME – HOLINESS & RIGHTEOUSNESS

If I've messed my life up, is it possible to become clean?

When an outdoorsman snags big game or makes a great catch that is not the end of his or her work. There are a few more things to be done before it is finished. Hunters bring their field-dressed game home or to a butcher, and fishermen bring their catch home to clean it so it can be used as it was intended. Cleaning the game can be just as intense and time-consuming as getting the game. It is the last thing an outdoorsman must do to enjoy the fruits of his or her labor.

When a hunter snags a deer, the deer is tagged and field-dressed, so it can be inspected by game wardens to determine the health and population of the herds. Some hunters choose to skin and butcher their game themselves, and others choose to take it to a butcher.

When fishermen bring home a big catch of fish, the fish must be scaled and cleaned to be stored or eaten. Some ways to prepare fish are filleting, separating the prime meat from the fish and skin, which is best for frying. Some fish are gutted and left whole. The more fish you catch, the longer it takes to clean them. Once the fish are clean they can be enjoyed.

Just as the outdoorsman needs to clean his game, God cleans Christians after they put their trust in Him. God's cleaning process is called holiness and righteousness. If you surrender to the Lord Jesus, **God begins to clean you from the inside out.** In a sense, God field dresses you when you accept Jesus as Lord and He removes all that junk that was within. People who may have been messed up, stressed out, broken-down, and wretched sinners, could come to Christ and He will make them holy and righteous children of God. They can be cleaned and made useful for God just like game is cleaned to be made useful to the outdoorsman.

Ephesians 4:24 says, "Put on the new man, which after God is created in righteousness and true holiness." When an outdoorsman gets his game or catches his catch, he takes his prize out of one environment and brings it into a new environment. He brings it from the field to freezer or from the water to the plate. God does the same thing with those who put their trust in Him. He takes them out of an environment of sin and brings them into a new environment of His Kingdom. The Lord takes sinners who were against Him, washes their sin away, and makes them holy and clean. The new standard for your new life in God is Jesus. When Jesus is your Lord, you are made holy the moment you accept Him into your heart. God continues to work in you as you follow after Him.

Luke 1:74-75 reveals that Christ followers have been rescued from the clutches of their enemies. Once rescued, they can serve God without fear in holiness and righteousness all their days. God gives believers a new nature, the nature of Jesus. He equips them with everything they need to follow Him successfully. He changes their course from destruction and death to life. God continually works in His children to lead, guide, and direct them in doing His will. God is amazing. He transforms sinners into saints when they surrender to Him by removing the filth and making them holy. They continue to be holy as they live by faith in God.

Just as the outdoorsman perfects his skill in whatever outdoor activities he participates in, believers in Christ perfect their holiness in the fear of God (2 Corinthians 7:1). A believer continues to develop in holiness as he honors, reveres, and respects God, His Word, His kingdom, His Spirit, His equipment and His people. God has cleansed your life from sin, and He desires for you to be holy for He is holy (1 Peter 1:15-16). Let God's cleaning process continue in your life so you can be useful to Him always.

CHAPTER 18
GETTING THE RIGHT LICENSE – AUTHORITY OF THE BELIEVER

Does a believer in Jesus Christ as Lord really have authority to do His work?

State and federal governments manage wildlife, maintain conservation, and keep people safe by regulating outdoor activities like hunting, fishing, and trapping through licensing. A license legally empowers, authorizes, and permits an outdoorsman to go after game in its season according to the limits of the license granted. These permits are not difficult to obtain and are helpful to keep everything operating smoothly, to ensure that wildlife populations are growing at a steady pace, and help maintain their existence for generations to come. Outdoorsmen may apply for licenses that they qualify for in order to do what they love.

If hunting was not regulated it could be disastrous to wildlife, humanity, and the environment. Animals would quickly become extinct if there were no limits imposed on the number that could be taken. Human injury and casualty would increase because there would be some people who would be careless and reckless hunters. Private property would no longer be private if no rules existed to protect it. The environment would be unbalanced due to the loss of species, and disease could rise. Be thankful that the licenses that are required for these outdoor activities are in place to prevent such bad things from happening.

Just as a license permits an outdoorsman to hunt, fish, and trap, a relationship with Jesus Christ permits His followers to exercise authority in the name of Jesus. The authority of the believer, in Christ Jesus, enables him or her to proclaim God's Word in the earth to bring salvation, healing, and deliverance, to defeat the enemy, and to be able to live a victorious life. Having faith in the name of Jesus and boldly declaring His name with your mouth is how you exercise your authority.

It is one thing to know that you have authority to do something, but it is another thing to know how to properly use that authority you have been granted. It is one thing to have a hunting license, but it is another thing to demonstrate you are a wise and safe hunter. Christ followers need to know how to use the name of Jesus just like a hunter needs to know how to properly use his weapon. Every believer in Christ Jesus has been given the authority to use Jesus' name, and His name is used to accomplish His purposes.

There is a story in Acts 3 that demonstrates one way believers can exercise authority in the earth. Peter and John, licensed disciples of Jesus, met a lame man at the entrance of the temple they were about to enter. This man sat there begging for money. Peter looked at the lame man and said, "Look at us." The lame man attentively looked at Peter and John expecting to receive something from them. Peter boldly declared to the lame man, "In the name of Jesus Christ of Nazareth, rise up and walk." Peter took the man by his hand, lifted him up, and immediately his legs and feet received strength. The lame man was no longer lame for he stood up, leaped, and walked in the temple with Peter and John. All the people who witnessed this were amazed at what happened.

Peter quickly let all the people know by whose authority

this miracle occurred. He said it was the name of Jesus, the faith of Jesus, and faith in His name that made the lame man strong. This is an amazing example of how believers can use and operate in the authority they have been given by Jesus.

The temple officials were very disturbed that Peter and John taught and preached about Jesus' resurrection from the dead. So they put them in jail. Even though you may be licensed or authorized to do something, people who are not familiar with who authorized you may question your license.

The leaders and the workers of the temple interrogated Peter and John about their authority. Peter was very outspoken and bold about the fact that it was Jesus Christ of Nazareth, Who authorized him and John to perform this miracle. Peter stated that there was only one name that could bring salvation, the name of Jesus. The officials saw their boldness, and the man who was healed, and could not deny what had happened.

The officials tried to regulate what Peter and John could preach by commanding them not to speak nor teach in the name of Jesus. The only one who can regulate what you preach or teach is the one who authorized you. Peter and John plainly told those officials that they were obeying God, not men. Their license did not come from earthly authority, but from God. You must be confident in the authority you have like Peter and John were.

Peter and John operated according to the license that Jesus issued to them. They proclaimed God's Word, and brought salvation, healing, and deliverance to this lame man and many others. The enemy could not stop them or prevent them from doing what they did even by intimidating them. They also had faith in their authorizing agent Jesus, and when their license was closely examined and questioned by men, they passed the test. You can operate in your authority just like they did.

Outdoorsmen apply for licenses with the proper authorities. A believer in Christ Jesus, who accepts Jesus as Lord and follows Him closely, is automatically authorized by the Lord Himself to do His work in the earth. Heaven is the issuing agency that gives permission to believers to represent heaven on earth. Your license to use the name of Jesus lasts as long as you walk with the Lord. Get licensed today, invite Jesus into your heart and accept Him as your Lord and Savior.

CHAPTER 19
CALLING THE GAME IN – ASSEMBLING A TEAM

How can I hear God's Call

Hunting involves a lot more than just going out into the woods with a weapon and returning home with an animal strapped to your vehicle. The hunter must devise the right strategy to attract an animal into his range. To do this, he appeals to the animal's senses. A hunter can use decoys - a fake man-made animal - to appeal to an animal's sense of sight to draw it in. Many hunters scent their own clothing with something their prey will find attractive. Finally, a hunter can appeal to the animal's sense of hearing by making sounds that it is familiar with. These sounds are called hunting calls.

Hunting calls are noises hunters make to attract specific animals. These calls can be made with a hunter's own hands and mouth, or he can use homemade devices, store-bought devices, or electronic devices. There many techniques and calls a hunter can use.

Animals each make unique sounds to their species. There are many reasons that animals make different sounds: finding their young, marking territory, locating a mate, warning other animals and humans to stay away, alerting other animals of the presence of a predator, and signaling distress. Different animals are attracted to different sounds.

Hunting calls are a lot like musical instruments – they require serious practice to master. In my own life, I have used a squirrel call, a duck call, a goose call, and the rattling of deer antlers to attract animals to where I was. A hunter must learn the right technique that each type of call requires. Using a hunting call in the wrong way can prevent the right animal from coming to you and it may attract the wrong animal to where you are. When using a hunting call, practice to perfect the sound.

For many years, my father, a few friends and I, would make an annual tip to Southern Illinois to hunt geese. The clubs we hunted at began to require hunters to hunt with guides. These guides were expert callers who could literally call geese very close to the blind we hunted in. One day, geese were flying overhead very high. The guide began to work and call the geese in. He made different sounds come out of the call. After a short time, geese flew within range and we each got our limit, which was two geese, per hunter, per day, very quickly. It was amazing to see the guide call in the geese. The call made the difference in our hunt.

How does calling in game relate to Christianity? Christians respond to the calls that come from Jesus Christ. The Lord Jesus calls people out of darkness, He calls them into a relationship with Him, He calls them to work for Him and He calls people gather together for His divine purposes. When the Lord calls, He appeals to our senses. God appealed to Moses' sight by using a bush that was on fire, yet was not being burned. Once God had Moses' attention, He could speak to Moses and tell him what He wanted him to do (Exodus 3). God appealed to Abraham's ears because the Bible does not say he saw anything, but he certainly heard what God said to him (Genesis 12:1-9). Jesus appealed to the emotions of two disciples who walked along a road after the resurrection of Jesus. They claimed their hearts burned within them while Jesus talked with them (Luke 24:32).

Throughout the Bible, God would gather His people together with a trumpet call. The trumpet would be a signal to gather for important things like special celebrations, a guide to set them on the right course, or an announcement to gather for war (Joshua 6:4). These blasts would be long or short, different pitch, or several blasts together for several times. The different blasts would bring God's people together for different reasons and they would respond to the different sounds. When you hear God's call, be sure you respond to it promptly.

Today, God is still inviting people to be part of His team and His family. Jesus is a good shepherd, who still calls sheep to Himself and leads them out of sin into eternal life (John 10:3). Ever since God created this world, He has been gathering a team to carry on His work. He calls individuals just like you. When God calls, answer it and obey His instructions.

Jesus is planning to return to the earth again. He is going to use a trumpet sound that believers in Him will hear and gather together to be with Him forever (Matthew 24:31). The trumpet of God will alert His people that the King of kings is arriving. 1 Corinthians 15:52 calls this trumpet "the last trumpet." Its blast will be so powerful it will raise the dead (1 Thessalonians 4:15-16). You can be ready now by accepting and following Jesus as Lord so you will be ready when that last trumpet sounds.

We hope you have enjoyed the analogies that are in this book. It is our desire to help you progress on your spiritual journey and to discover the God of creation through spiritual truths that are paralleled in outdoors activities. Be God's outdoorsman and practice these truths in your life. You will have great joy in following the Lord as you read and study His Word, allow His Holy Spirit to lead, guide and direct you and do what you were created to do. May God richly bless you in following the Lord.

BIBLIOGRAPHY

Biblesoft's New Exhaustive Strong's Numbers and Concordance with Expanded Greek-Hebrew Dictionary. Copyright © 1994, 2003 Biblesoft, Inc. and International Bible Translators, Inc.

Chapter 13: from - Nelson's Illustrated Bible Dictionary, Copyright I1986, Thomas Nelson Publishers

Chapter 19: MUSICAL INSTRUMENTS

The shophar, or trumpet, was basically a signaling instrument, used to assemble the army (Judg 3:27; 1 Sam 13:3), to sound an attack (Job 39:24-25), and to sound an alarm (Jer 6:1; Amos 3:6).

The ram's horn signaled war and peace, the new moon, the beginning of the Sabbath, approaching danger, and the death of a dignitary.

The sound of the shophar could be heard from a great distance (Ex 19:16,19). It can produce only the first two tones of the musical scale and those not very accurately.

from Nelson's Illustrated Bible Dictionary, Copyright (c)1986, Thomas Nelson Publishers

As above intimated, the Lord commanded Moses to make two trumpets of beaten silver, for the purpose of calling the people together when they were to decamp (Num 10). They chiefly used these trumpets, however, to proclaim the beginning of the civil year, the beginning of the sabbatical year (Lev 23:24; Num 29:1), and the beginning of the jubilee (Lev 25:9,10).

from McClintock and Strong Encyclopedia, Electronic Database. Copyright © 2000, 2003 by Biblesoft, Inc. All rights reserved.

ABOUT THE AUTHORS

Douglas Pyszka

Douglas Pyszka is passionate about helping people from all walks of life to find their inheritance in the Word of God. He is an author and international speaker. He is also Lead Pastor at Victory Christian Fellowship, Palmyra PA. He is a graduate of Rhema Bible Training College and Lee University. He is married to Fiona and has two sons, Gabriel and Josiah. He and his family currently reside in Central Pennsylvania.

Nelson Rhoads

Nelson H. Rhoads is passionate about bringing people to salvation. His desire is for people to really know the compassion of Jesus so that they may know why Jesus did the things He did for us. He is a graduate of PA Minister Association and Rhema Correspondence Bible School. He has served in multiple capacities in the church. His favorite service is teaching the youth and worshiping God with his guitar. Nelson is an avid outdoorsman, a skilled carpenter, and a passionate worship musician. He is married to Nadine and is blessed to have four stepchildren.